DAILY DEVOTIONAL series

WISDOM HUNTERS

SEEKING GOD IN THE PSALMS

90 READINGS FOR INSPIRATION, INTIMACY & INSTRUCTION

BOYD BAILEY

Published by **Wisdom Hunters, inc.**

Scripture taken from the Holy Bible, New International Version®, NIV®, Copyright © 1973, 1978, 1984 by International Bible Society. Used by permission of Zondervan. All rights reserved.

Cover and book design by **truth in advertising** (atlanta, GA 404.798.6309 www.truthinadvertising.net)

Wisdom Hunters, Inc.
PO Box 800062
Roswell, GA 30075

Visit us at **www.WisdomHunters.com**

The Wisdom Hunters name and logo are trademarks of Wisdom Hunters, LLC.

ISBN: 978-1-4507-9154-0

DEDICATION

TO OUR FOUR
FAITHFUL DAUGHTERS:

REBEKAH

RACHEL

BETHANY

ANNA GRACE

WHOSE KING IS ENTHRALLED
BY THEIR BEAUTY
PSALM 45:11

ACKNOWLEDGEMENTS

Thank you **Pete** and **Debbie Ochs**
for your generosity that made this book possible.

Thank you **Billy Graham**
for modeling a life that daily drinks from the Psalms.

Thank you **Paul Ryden**
for your expert editing.

Thank you **Michael Dolinger**
for your creative design.

Thank you **Jonathan Bolden**
for being an encourager and process thinker.

Thank you **Wisdom Hunters Board of Directors**
for your love, prayers and accountability.

Thank you **Gwynne Maffett**
for being our Wisdom Hunters Prayer Warrior.

TESTIMONIES

Experiencing God stories from the Wisdom Hunters devotional writings:

Servant Leadership
A few weeks ago you printed a wonderful article on leadership. It was probably the finest summary of traits that we should all aspire to obtain. I have shared this article with many folks in my organization and have had a number of positive interactions as a result of your article. One person in Geneva, Switzerland even decided to receive your articles every day. Thanks so much for keeping God's principles before us in a practical and challenging way.
– Bob

A Humble Husband
You have written an article that has started an invigorating debate among my friends. How exciting to stir up such a wonderful debate. Your research is very useful. Thank you.

Loved to Learn
Thank you for this message. My husband read it to me when I was almost ready to quit trying! We are losing our home, my husband had to go on disability, and we are moving. It has been my desire to become a public speaker and my husbands to be a minister but it seems as if my dreams have been dashed so often. This encouraged me! God Bless
– Malinda

Failure is Not Final
It is very timely that this was today's encouragement. Just yesterday I was really upset over my failures. I do not have to live in condemnation about it. It is just one more step that I have to take. One more step forward. One more moment with God holding me close.
– Alexandria

Where I Want my Heart to Wander

I am deeply moved by this meditation and I am grateful that you were obedient to our loving God and Father when you wrote it. In my opinion, it takes great courage to be transparent and your willingness to be so truthful is truly an encouragement and inspiration to me. It also reminds me that all of us are a work in progress and you have given me permission not to be so hard on myself when I get a bit off course. You are so right when you said that you "write out of real life to real people about a real God." and for that I wish to simply say "Thank you." May the blessings that you have poured into my life by writing this meditation be multiplied back to you a thousand fold!
– Roberta

Temporary Setbacks

Wow! This is just the food I need for my spirit! I was led to close my dream business early this year, and thought now what? My flesh had given up on my passion and thought that I needed to find a different field. After searching in the world I felt soooo lost and not so confident. But God...He put my song back in my heart. This blog is just confirmation and what I have been asking God for. Thank you sooo much! I have a new perspective on why I am at the place where I am in my life. God is definitely up to something and I am excited about what He is doing and going to do. His strength has made me strong! Glory be to God!
– Tolanda

Reassuring words

Dear Boyd Bailey, I really needed to hear this today and I am praising God right now for speaking to me through you! Directly! Now I have more to pray for and work out! God Bless You and keep you. Love you Boyd.

True Love

I wish to thank you for blessing me and my family with these BEAUTIFUL doses of TRUE LOVE!!! Blessed
– Cindy

A Working Mother

This was so affirming for me. Thank you Lord for giving me what I need at the right moments in my life.
– Kim

TESTIMONIES

Value Highly
*Thank-you for your daily devotionals they have encouraged me each morning.
God is so good and His word will direct our paths if we take the time to read it.
God bless you all for the wonderful work you are doing. Sincerely*
– Linda

A Humble Leader
*I have really enjoyed reading Wisdom Hunters in the morning before work,
I have actually shared it with my store director in that I am in a field of retail
and serving. My leadership team as well as the partners who work alongside
me would so benefit from these words of wisdom. I can see that leadership
initiates servitude as well as humility, the store's morale and our customer
relations would prosper. All parties would benefit and the light of Christ
would shine in our small town. The impact to the community as a whole
would be awesome and encouraging. Thank you for being obedient
and following in what the Lord has asked you to do.*

Unresolved Pain
*I cannot thank you enough for today's dose. Oddly enough, I just started
subscribing this week. I guess God knew this was coming and I needed this.
Often these pains are lived with alone, silently. Yet our Savior is the only one
who really needs to know. Today dose eloquently defined what I've been
searching to explain for over a year now. You have no idea how much
this will help, both outward as I minister with others and inward as
I heal deep wounds with thick scars. Thank you.*
– Kay

Righteous Resolve
*Thank you so much for these wonderful devotionals. God really speaks
to me through these. Have shared some with my children and friends.
Best devotionals I have ever had. God bless you.*
– Karen

PREFACE

Seeking God in the Psalms is a collection of the reader's favorites from the daily Wisdom Hunters email devotionals written between 2008-2009. These flow from my heart as I have wept and rejoiced with the Lord in my daily quiet times. I pray the Lord will use these writings to bring inspiration, intimacy and instruction to your relationship with Him.

A Servant in Christ,

Boyd Bailey

boyd@wisdomhunters.com

Books & Devotionals by BOYD BAILEY

E-book Devotionals

Infusion – a 90-day devotional

Seeking Daily the Heart of God – a 365-day devotional

Wisdom for Love – a 30–day devotional

Wisdom for Graduates – a 30-day devotional

Wisdom for Mothers – a 30-day devotional

Wisdom for Fathers – a 30-day devotional

Print books

Infusion

Seeking Daily the Heart of God

All books and devotionals available at **wisdomhunters.com**

INTRODUCTION

The Psalms are my default to experience God in all His glory. They describe the Lord as a secure refuge and cool place to rest under the shadow of His love. Righteous refreshment is found in God's green grass beside still waters—care from our loving Great Shepherd for His sheep. Indeed, there is sound security that accompanies a trusting soul.

The Psalms invite peace and reveal pain. The 150 chapters of truth and transparency communicate trust in the Lord and struggles with sin and distrust. Some seeking souls are tortured by fear and doubt, while others are quieted under the calming hand of Christ. Fortunately, faith eventually wins out for most—though getting there is not always easy!

Most of the Psalms are birthed from an autobiography of seeking the Lord. Moses, David and the Psalmist each describe their unique experience with God. They are so intensely personal that you feel their emotion gradually bubble up from hurt and anger, or immediately explode into praise and adoration. These writings are raw and real in their appeal, so much that at times I bow my head and pray a Psalm, as it better bares my heart.

The Psalms can be described as songs, hymns, canticles, poems and prayers. It's out of these diverse writing styles that a tantalizing truth awaits to capture a willing heart. We live many times with a bias of meeting our felt needs—hence the powerful intersection of intimacy we experience with the Lord—when with humble heart we meditate on a Psalm.

Do you question the existence of God? Do you sometimes wonder why good people suffer and bad people prosper? Have crushing circumstances made you mad at yourself, God and others? Or are you at the pinnacle of pleasure and success—being tempted to take the credit? Are you in need of fresh soul care in rest, reflection, praise and worship?

INTRODUCTION

Regardless of where you find yourself on the continuum of following Christ, you can engage with eternity in the Psalms. Perhaps you once burned with passion for God, but over time life has lowered your enthusiasm for godly living. The Psalms are a reliable remedy to reignite your fiery faith. Maybe adversity has beat up your emotions and left you alone—your heavenly Father will meet you through these love letters just for you.

At times my doubts drive me to my knees with the Book of Psalms open before me—I read and pray over each word and phrase—searching for a divine antidote for my fears. Then the Holy Spirit—like the Rosetta stone interprets ancient Egyptian hieroglyphics—takes my willing heart, and clarifies God's purpose for my life. He uses His word to comfort and convict my heart—and to instruct my head. I forget, but He lovingly reminds.

So, use these simple writings as an excuse to get before the Lord and let Him love on you. These reflections are not an end in themselves, but the starting point of where God wants to take you in your faith walk. Confess your need for Him and He will not disappoint you.

"Teach me your way, LORD, that I may rely on your faithfulness;
give me an undivided heart, that I may fear your name" (Psalm 86:11).

TITLE INDEX

TITLE INDEX

TITLE INDEX

REFUGE IN HIM

Blessed are all who take refuge in Him.
Psalm 2:12b

Outside of Christ we are refugees in need of a refuge. Our soul seeks asylum in Almighty God. Our spirit is on a search for security and peace. It is refuge in God that we want deep down within our inner most desires. Otherwise we wander around earth un-tethered to truth. We are induced into thinking things are ok outside of our Savior's care. But there is something more significant that comes by slowing down and investigating our own authenticity. Refugees need a place of safety and trust. It is in refuge with Him that we can believe Him. There is an intimacy with Jesus that invites us into refuge.

Even if your faith is as slender as a spider's thread you can still trust in Jesus. It is the object of your faith that matters more than the amount of your faith. His refuge is not just reserved for the robust of faith. It is especially available to those of us that are flailing away in faithless fear. We have lost our way and we need to a wise weigh station to ferret out our faith. It is in refuge with Him that we are blessed with clarity and conviction. God is our refuge and God is our strength. He is a very present help in trouble. Therefore we will not fear, but will believe that the very best is found by faith in Him. Hope exists.

He is our refuge when hope seems extinct. He is our refuge when financial requirements are ravishing our resources. He is our refuge when people we depend on are nowhere to be found. He is our refuge when health issues hound our heart. He is our refuge when fear knocks at the door and courts our courage. He is our refuge when our marriage hangs in the balance. He is our refuge when work pressures pulsate in our mind and awake us at night. He is our refuge when all seems to be going wrong. He is our refuge when all seems to be going right. His refuge is required regardless of our circumstances. During the good and bad times we need to rest and refuel under the shadow and wisdom of His almighty wings. It is in refuge and relationship with God that His blessings abound.

We are blessed when we find refuge with our Creator. The Almighty aids us with wisdom and understanding when we take the time to listen to His instruction. Our prayer over His Word provides a ton of illuminating insight. The place of refuge holds up truth and casts out lies. It is a place of clarity and conviction. This is a blessing. Stability is another blessing from resting in His refuge. Our world rocks around us. Instability is the only insulation infidels care to offer. But we have a rock in our Lord.

He is solid and dependable. There is nothing about our Savior that is shaky. He is not a suspension bridge that sways with the winds of the world's unpredictability. He is a concrete crossover to the shore of peace and calm. He cannot be shaken by strife or sin because He is Holy God. He is our rock when relationships are rocky. This is a blessing. Lastly we are blessed in our refuge with Him by reassurance. He whispers lovingly, "Its ok. I am with you. I will never leave you. You are mine. I am yours. Therefore hold me tight and we will walk together through 'thick and thin." It's in refuge with Him that we are refreshed and rejuvenated. Go there often. He bestows blessings in refuge with Him!

REFLECTIONS

_____

_____

_____

_____

_____

_____

2

PEACE OF MIND

I lie down and sleep; I wake again, because the LORD sustains me.
I will not fear the tens of thousands drawn up against me on every side.
Psalm 3:5-6

Peace of mind comes from our Master Jesus. He is the master at putting our mind at ease with His eternal perspective. It is trust in Him that gives us tranquil thoughts. Without His peace we worry and fret. A peace-less mind is paralyzed by the thought of everything going awry. What can go wrong will go wrong because the odds are stacked against us. Without the peace of Christ we find ourselves with an overwhelming sense of dread, even despair. However His peace transcends our tentative trust. It bolsters our belief in God. Our Savior extends a sweet sense of peace. In Christ we have peace of mind like a bee in a hive or a dove in the ark. His helmet of salvation produces peaceful thoughts.

Jesus is not stingy with His peace. He gives it liberally and lovingly (John 14:27). Beware of the fleeting peace the world offers. It is a very cheap substitute. The world's peace is circumstantial. His peace transcends circumstances. The world's peace is temporal. His peace is eternal. The world's peace leads you to escape from God and reality. His peace leads you to engage with both. The world's peace produces a limited perspective. His peace results in a robust and real view of life. The world's peace has the residue of guilt and bondage. His peace leaves you forgiven and free. The world's peace can not remove fear. His peace overcomes fear with hope. The world's peace is based on feelings. His peace is grounded in faith. Therefore wisdom receives His peace.

Once you apply the peace of Christ you have peace of mind. Peace of mind gives you a platform for living purposively. Because you live purposively and peacefully you garner influence with others. People are attracted to the peaceful. They want to learn how to find and apply peace to their life circumstances. Your friends or family may not acknowledge it, but your peace is proof of God's existence. Peace is a powerful apologetic for the Almighty. Your calmness during crisis can only be explained by Christ. Because you lean on Him others want to lean on you. You are a 'lean two' for your Lord. So use prayerfully this platform of peace for ministry. People will line up for peace of mind.

Lastly use your peace of mind as a gauge for God's will. If you have peace proceed, but if you lack peace heed. God's peace is a green light to go forward. The absence of His peace is a red light to refrain. Therefore be sensitive to the Spirit's peaceful prodding to go or stay. Either way you are ok as long as the Lord's peace is preeminent. Peace gives you a state of mind that is able to think clearly and wisely. Peace positions you for right thinking. Do not impulsively barrel ahead without peace of mind. Emotions can play tricks on our trust and good

REFLECTIONS

_____

_____

_____

_____

_____

_____

3

CHOSEN BY GOD

Know that the Lord has set apart the godly for himself;
the Lord will hear when I call to him.
Psalm 4:3

God chooses His children for Himself. Our relationship with our Lord is all about Him. It is all about His desires, His pleasures, His vision, His goals and His will. When we came to God we came empty handed clinging only to the cross of Christ. So in our surrender to our Savior we emptied ourselves and received Jesus. We went from self-sufficient to God dependent. We went from flesh patterns to spiritual habits. We went from ungodly to godly. We went from an impersonal relationship with a distant God to an intimate relationship with our Heavenly Father up close and personal. God chose us for Himself. Now in our engagement with eternity we want what God wants. Our passions have been purged from the temporal to the eternal. We get excited over what excites God.

Furthermore, He wants us to know and not forget these basic tenets of Christianity. He knows we need to know. He knows that we need to know because we forget and revert back to beliefs that rival God's ownership of our lives. Because He owns us, He owns everything about us. You may be struggling with traveling overseas for the sake of His cause. But Jesus commands are clear that we are to go into all the world and make disciples. Or you may be too busy to build a relationship with your neighbors. But our sensitive Savior implores us to love our neighbors. Our words may say one thing but our behavior is what brands us. What can we do today to set ourselves apart as His? Our distinctive may to reflect a patient attitude, a caring comment or sinless anger toward hypocrisy. We are at His disposal to carry our His desires. This is His expectation.

Moreover God offers a clear channel of communication for His children. He hears when we call to Him. Prayer is not passive for our Heavenly Father. He is interested in our intense circumstances and our heart felt fears. Because we are His, He listens to and answers our prayers. It is not always an answer as we think it needs to be answered. He defines His will for us as much with his answers of 'no' as He does with His answers of 'yes'. Our prayers are a response to the love, respect, dependency and trust we have in our Heavenly Father. Because we are His we come to Him often as does a healthy relationship with a child and parent. We have no need to fear for our Heavenly Father is near. He is near to listen and to love. He is near to forgive and heal. He is a prayer away.

The more we constantly converse with Christ surely we will speak all the more boldly to men. Prayer is a purging and a preparation. It is God's platform to launch us out into fields that are ripe for harvest. It is a preparation for engagement in the lives of people. Prayer fills us with love so we can be emptied of love. We are chosen by God. What He chooses He makes holy. We are godly because we are God's. It is holiness that makes us fit to live with holy God forever. Without holiness we cannot see our Savior (Hebrews 12:14). Boldness follows seeing Jesus. Because He was poured out we are sold out!

REFLECTIONS

_____

_____

_____

_____

_____

_____

4

TROUBLEMAKERS

The trouble he causes recoils on himself;
his violence comes down on his own head.
Psalm 7:15

Troublemakers tend to self-destruct. There is no need to get worked up over their acts of deception. They are dishonest. They lie when the truth will suffice. The harm they intend to inflict on others comes back to hurt them. Troublemakers attempt to discredit those they are jealous of and in the process discredit themselves. Troublemakers conceive elaborate plans with evil intent. It is all about them and their agenda. They can easily tell you one thing and do another. With delight they can 'push your buttons' to get what they want. With a straight face they can make up stories to embolden their position. Deception is a means to an end. In their mind good outcomes justify a polluted process. It doesn't matter how you get to the goal as long as you reach the goal.

Beware of troublemakers but do not urge them on with too much attention. Keep an eye on them but do not be consumed by them. Stand up to them in the right spirit without crushing their spirit. They are totally insecure and fearful, but are afraid to admit their insecurities. Because their acceptance is based on performance they are always looking for ways to impress others. They miss the point that we are totally and unconditionally accepted in Christ. He is our stability for security. It is not what we do that keeps us secure it is who we are and who's we are. In Christ we have all we need. We do not have to impress others we just need to be who we are in Him. The fruit of the Spirit will do the talking for us. People are impressed with follow through not fancy but false promises.

Trust God with troublemakers. You are not their judge and jury. He can handle them in His timing and in His way. We have our own sins to confess and repent of on a regular basis. Our sins may not be as blatant but they are still present. We may not sin in as pronounced manner as a troublemaker; nonetheless we still struggle with dishonesty and deception. It may be on a smaller scale but we still weight in as ones who struggle with being a troublemaker. So let's contrast the life of a troublemaker by being a blessing maker. Let's be a blessing instead of a curse. Let's extend consolation instead of consternation. Let's focus on giving instead of taking. Let's be a solace instead of a pain. Let's serve instead of being served. Let's encourage instead of discouraging. Kill them with kindness and watch God turn their hearts toward Him.

Furthermore, pray for troublemakers to trust God. Pray they will offer to Him their lives for His glory. Replace gossip with prayers to God on their behalf. At the right time and in the right way, help them understand their destructive ways. Otherwise they will destroy themselves. They prepare destruction for themselves by preparing themselves for destruction. Be a catalyst of Christ's to guide them away from this path of self-destruction. Be willing to spend money on a coach who can give them objective feedback and a reality check. But do everything out of love and respect in the context of relationship. Give them the respect they never had and they may begin to respect themselves. God's grace can change troublemakers into blessing makers. We are proof!

REFLECTIONS

_____

_____

_____

_____

_____

_____

5

LIPS OF CHILDREN

From the lips of children and infants you have ordained praise
because of your enemies, to silence the foe and the avenger.
Psalm 8:2

The lips of children lift up the greatness of God in praise and adoration. They do not know any better than to believe God and take Him at His word. They are trusting and pure in their devotion. It is the children that embraced the coronation of Christ in His triumph entry into Jerusalem. They shouted "Hosanna in the highest" while the proud religious leaders were indignant (Matthew 21:15). Humility praises Jesus, but pride is silent. Humility invites Jesus, but pride is threatened by Jesus. Humility wants to sit in His lap, but pride rejects His love and affection. Children remind us of the God we have forgotten. We get so sophisticated with our Savior that we miss Him. We use to cry out to Him in gratitude over His overwhelming grandeur, but somewhere along the way have taken Him for granted. Children remind us of God's greatness. This is their lot.

Children live in a constant state of dependency. They depend on their parents for food, clothing and shelter. Children look to their parents to teach them about God and religion. Hobbies like fishing, hunting, camping, ballet, chess, gymnastics, drama, golf, tennis, football, baseball, basketball, hockey, music and art become a committed interest of children with their parents prodding and encouragement. Parents are a plethora of resources for their children. Boys and girls depend on mom and dad for direction around what they do well and how they can excel best. Parents are a warehouse of wisdom for their offspring. Children who are compliant in learning from and depending on their parents are successful. They-- maybe unknowingly– build a solid foundation for living.

Our relationship with God is no different. We are His children in desperate need of His direction. We may spurn His discipline at times, but we come back because we know He is what we need. We need His wisdom. We need His forgiveness. We need His comfort, love and hope. We need his perspective to be able to work effectively with people. We need His security found in Christ. We need His courage in crisis. We need His grace in the middle of criticism. We need His humility to defeat pride. Christians who succeed the most are totally and utterly dependent on Christ. Otherwise our pride drives us to self-sufficiency and shallow or patronizing praises of God. His greatness decreases as ours increases. Therefore we re-crown Him King daily. By faith we step away from the throne of our life and humbly bow at His feet, as He sits enthroned and worthy of all praise.

Children are the conscience of adults. They remind us of our dependency on Jesus. We are but a grain of sand on the seashore of humanity. Jesus is Lord of all and we serve and worship Him alone. The lips of children naturally lift up the glory of God. And we do so supernaturally by the power of the Holy Spirit. We cannot keep shut because of His lavish love and the abundant grace He pours forth on the faithful. It's in our childlike faith that God reveals Himself. But He hides the very same from the wisdom of the world (Luke 10:21). You are God's child; therefore praise and adore His majestic name!

REFLECTIONS

_____

_____

_____

_____

_____

_____

6

NAÏVE EXPECTATIONS

He says to himself, "Nothing will shake me;
I'll always be happy and never have trouble.
Psalm 10:6

There is no such thing as a trouble free life. This is naïve, presumptive and proud. Pride does this. It instills false confidence and unrealistic expectations. A man thinks himself immutable and omnipotent to conclude he will always be free from adversity. Jesus said just the opposite. He taught we are not of this world therefore the world will hate us (John 15:19). This is not an invitation to a life of ease. It is a guarantee for conflict. The naïve pronounces an out of control optimism not based in reality. His house is built on the sand and he will experience loss when the first winds of suffering blow over his life. Pride sets us up for a fall (Proverbs 16:18). There is no way to totally shield ourselves from pain.

We who are overly secure are never safe. There is no opulent home or outrageous bank account that can keep us from never suffering. Wealth sets us up for disappointment. Boastings are not buttresses and self confidence is a sorry security. Our confidence is in Christ not in our ever changing life of uncertainty. He is a perfect purpose outside of our self. He has a much greater and much more massive meaning. We can expect great things from Him because He is great. He is immovable and immutable. We vacillate. We change. We struggle. We doubt. We fear. This is why we cast our lot with the Lord. When life happens and the bottom falls out we have a solid foundation in our Savior.

Pride on the other hand brews naïve expectations. This is the ruin of fools. When they succeed their confidence bloats out of control. There needs to be a dose of humility that brings them back into the realities of everyday life. Indeed in your success do not seclude yourself from ordinary people. Make sure you engage with those who are still clearing their career path and muddling their way through marriage or struggling to raise kids. Engagement in the lives of others leads us to a more fulfilling life. It is in our success that we are set up to serve others. To give back is to govern like God. This is what He expects. Godly expectations lead us down the road of service and selflessness.

So instead of insulating our lives from all danger and risks we follow the lead of the Holy Spirit. We ask questions like, 'What does God think?' 'Will this opportunity contribute to my spiritual growth?' 'How does my spouse weight in?' 'What is best for my family?' 'What will give me the most leverage for the Lord?' We seek to align our expectations with eternity. It is an ongoing process of dying to ourselves and coming alive for the Lord. So do not become disillusioned in your discomfort.

"In fact, everyone who wants to live a godly life in Christ Jesus will be persecuted, while evil men and impostors will go from bad to worse, deceiving and being deceived (2 Timothy 3:12-13)". It is not a life of ease that we need to expect, but a life of obedience. Moreover do not expect money to be a cure all. More money applied to naïve expectations set us up for bitter disappointment. Instead expect great things from God. Trust Him in and with your troubles. These are expectations for the mature of faith. Wisdom aligns expectations with His. Expect this!

REFLECTIONS

_____

_____

_____

_____

_____

_____

7

STAND STEADFAST

In the Lord I take refuge. How then can you say to me:
'Flee like a bird to your mountain'.
Psalm 11:1

There is a time to stand steadfast and there is a time to flee. Make sure your motive for either is based on trust. Do not allow others to persuade you to run and hide when you need to stand and fight. Having faith in God may mean engaging in some uncomfortable activities. Don't run off just because you are afraid of being roughed up. Any body can leave but trust in God implores you to stay. Be aggressive with your agitators. Let them know that you will not be intimidated by false promises or bad advice. Beware of people whose counsel sounds right but it is wrapped in selfish motivations. They may want you to move on so they can move in. Others vie for your power because they lust for its influence. So stand steadfast in your Savior. Trust Jesus with this temptation to flee.

One of Satan's schemes is distrust. If he can get us to lose faith in our Heavenly Father then he can influence our decision making with foolish thoughts. Satan is patient. He knows a little incremental doubt can lead to a large amount of distrust. Bad advice can be deceptive on the surface. It may even sound like your counselors have your best interest in mind. After all with a tinge of sincerity they communicate 'worry' over your safety or your reputation. But in reality they are really mocking you and God. Why would someone want you to run away from trusting God unless they had something in mind for themselves? This moment of decision is an opportunity for your faith to intersect with God's faithfulness. If you run you will miss refuge in Jesus. Therefore stand steadfast.

Stability comes from standing steadfast with your Savior. However distrust is like a silly bird. It flutters here and there with no aim other than reacting to ever distraction. There is nothing significant about a sparrow running scarred. It is but a dot of distrust on a mountain with the masses. Anybody can run and hide in the face of difficult people or challenging circumstances. Like the religious leaders who made fun of Jesus, some may say, 'He trusts in God. Let God rescue him now if he wants him...' (Matthew 27:43). Indeed some may blame God for the undeserving outcomes we are experiencing. But this unfair criticism only emboldens a strong faith that stands steadfast. Consider the source of your critics. Does their life reflect total trust, or is their faith one of convenience?

Moreover use this time of turmoil to trust the Lord even more. His calling has not changed. Stand steadfast. Stand steadfast in Him and you will stand steadfast in your marriage. Stand steadfast in Him and you will stand steadfast in your vocation. Stead steadfast in Him and you will stand steadfast in your purity. Stand steadfast in Him and you will stand steadfast in your friendship. Stand steadfast in Him and you will stand steadfast in your church. It is easy to leave when everyone else is fleeing from the carnage. Nevertheless we are convicted to stand steadfast and trust Him, even if we are the last one standing. Those we respect may even run, but we remain ever vigilant. Stand alone with the Almighty. Others will return. And you will be there to graciously great them. People need a rock of reason. Therefore stand on the rock of Jesus for their sake!

REFLECTIONS

_____

_____

_____

_____

_____

_____

8

FLAWLESS WORDS

And the words of the LORD are flawless, like silver refined
in a furnace of clay, purified seven times.
Psalm 12:6

The words of the Lord are flawless. There is no dross in Christ's conversation. Men may lie but He is the truth. Men may deceive but Jesus enlightens. Men may flatter but the Lord edifies. Men may boast but Jesus gives the glory to God. Words can be wonderful or terrible depending on their source. The words of the Lord are rooted in righteousness. There is no doubt when Deity makes a declaration of truth. What comes forth from the Lord's lips are from a mouth with 100% pure motives. You can trust what God says because He speaks without guile or guilt. His words are not vain but very appropriate and applicable. It is the words of heaven that make earth better. Indeed the words of the Lord have stood the test of time. They have been tried by fire and have come forth faithful.

The Holy Scriptures have not been without criticism and consternation. The Bible has been stripped of its miracles and added to by self appointed prophets. Even though Jesus warned there are severe consequences for adding to His word (Revelation 22:18). Furthermore God's Word does not need help. His words have survived the ravishing of faithless liberalism and loveless legalism. His Word has outlasted the cloak of the church within an ancient translation for none but the 'holy' to understand. The Lords words have been tried by the fire of falsehood, faithlessness, fear, forgetfulness and foreign gods. The Bible has been burned, belittled and ignored. Nonetheless: after the bias due diligence of skeptical and cynical men it still flourishes. The Holy Scriptures are translated into more languages today than ever in the history of mankind. It has stood the test of time.

So take the Lord's flawless words by faith. Read them daily and apply them moment by moment. Study them and struggle with them. Seek to understand the context of the Bible and why God chose to speak specific infallible words through fallible followers. The Holy Spirit is the author of the Holy Scriptures (2 Peter 1:21). The pen of men only moved under the instruction of divine inspiration. So we have a stewardship of truth. The Bible is our handbook for holiness and happiness. We steward it well when we honor it above our own wishful thinking. The words of the Lord are extremely valuable and not to be taken for granted. Therefore listen to the Lord often and listen expectantly.

We honor and value His words when we take them to heart. We do not listen to the Lord to fulfill an obligation. We listen for instructions in our obedience. We listen for encouragement. We listen for rebuke. We listen to the Lord's flawless words because we know we are loved by Him. We have infinite access to Wisdom. The clarity, cut, color and carat of Christ's words are flawless and invaluable. They are matchless compared to man's meager trinkets. We are wise when we make our words the words of Christ. Children speak the words of their parents. We mouth the language of our Lord. Our words grow in value as we speak His priceless promises. Then we have something to say!

REFLECTIONS

_____

_____

_____

_____

_____

_____

9

GRATEFUL FOR GOOD

I will sing to the Lord, for he has been good to me.
Psalm 13:6

God has been good to us. His goodness is liberal and long lasting. His goodness is far reaching. It extends to the embarrassment of failure and to the pride of success. His goodness is good. If we could eat the goodness of God it would satisfy our taste buds with trusting delight. Because He is God He is good. There is nothing bad that soils the character of our Savior. The salvation we have in Jesus is good. The comfort we have in Christ is good. The wisdom we gain by applying God's principles is good. His answers to prayer are good. His forgiveness is good. His grace is good. Heaven is good. God is so good to us. We can't help but exclaim His goodness in praise and adoration. We sing to the Lord because His goodness compels us. "Let the word of Christ dwell in you richly as you teach and admonish one another with all wisdom, and as you sing psalms, hymns and spiritual songs with gratitude in your hearts to God" (Colossians 3:16).

Gratitude gushes forth from a heart that has been tamed by the goodness of God. God has been good to us. The recognition of His goodness governs our gratitude. To the extent we remember how good God is to us; is the degree of appreciation we apply in our everyday life. His goodness to us draws out gratitude in spades. His goodness invites gratitude. Moreover He extends His goodness to us personally. It is not just one gigantic corporate application of goodness like a nation that allows freedom of religion and free enterprise. He applies His goodness to our individual situations, like a mother who prepares a delicious meal for her family. It may be He has given us a good job, good health, good sense, a good house and a good family. It is the grace of God that allows us to experience His goodness. When we linger under the cross of Christ we encounter the shade of His goodness. "God is so good. God is so good. God is so good. He's so good to me."

Therefore when we are under the bright light of God's goodness any influence of bad is blinded. Gratitude and a bad attitude cannot coexist. Take the time and list out what good things the Lord has done for you. Keep your list close by so when you are tempted to complain over trivial issues like traffic, another's tardiness, waiting in line or not getting what you want, you can apply gratitude. People world-wide who love Jesus and make one dollar a day do this all the time. They do not allow their circumstances or financial limitations determine their gratitude. They are grateful because of the goodness of God that governs their attitude and actions. Passion may possess an unbridled body, but patience controls a grateful soul. Indeed His goodness beckons us to be good.

Goodness gives off goodness. It rubs off on others. God's goodness infects us so we can infect others. We are 'carriers' for Christ. We are good to others because God has been good to us. Our goodness does not discriminate. We are good to others even when they are undeserving. This is the nature of God's goodness. Be patient with the one who doesn't deserve patience. Love the one who doesn't deserve love. Forgive the one who doesn't deserve forgiveness. This is good. This is what Jesus would do. Receive God's goodness. Apply it gratefully. He has been so extremely good to us!

REFLECTIONS

_____

_____

_____

_____

_____

_____

GOD IS PRESENT

*There they are, overwhelmed with dread, for God is present
in the company of the righteous.*
Psalm 14:5

God is present in your predicament. You do not have to pray, "God be with us". He is there already. He is there because He cares. He is there because you are extremely valuable to Him. God's cherishes His children. He loves to give His own good gifts (Matthew 7:11). His presence alone is a present. He is present to give wisdom. He is present to give you direction. He is present to give you courage. In His presence there is peace. Yet we sometimes act like our God is distant and disconnected from our discouragement. We would never say there is no God that would be foolish. But our unbelieving behavior acts like an atheist. We fret and we fear when our faith comes under fire. We are fragile. However God is near we have no need to fear. He is ever present.

God's presence is there to gives us calm and conviction. His peace is what propels us forward by faith. Do not give up on doing the right thing. Sinful compromise for short term satisfaction never ends well. Why put your family to risk by running after forbidden fruit? God has not left you. He does not wink at wicked deeds. He is right by your side to see you through this sinful temptation. Indeed the fear of God is the fruit of His presence. When we walk with Jesus we want to obey Jesus. The bed of adultery is repulsive when accompanied by the Almighty. He is present so don't go there. Being in the presence of holiness causes us to blush in the face of sin. His presence is a protection against foolish decisions. Just knowing the Lord is watching is a wake up call to wisdom.

His presence is made manifest in a company of Christ followers. It is in community that the Body of Christ is in full form. Sin pushes us to seclusion. It is an illusion to think we can isolate ourselves from Almighty God. But in authentic community there is no where to hide. It is in the presence of committed Christ followers that we feed our faith. Do not fight temptation alone. Tell someone. Reengage with the righteous. Early repentance rests in community but is deferred outside of the caring confrontation from those who care. Community goes after its own. It does more than pray. It pursues. Being in the presence of the righteous is the presence of God personified. This keeps us accountable. This keeps us pure. This keeps our perspective in reality. This keeps us encouraged.

Therefore by staying in the presence of God-fearing followers we stay engaged with God. This time of engagement with others facilitates our alone time with our Heavenly Father. Stay hard after your Heavenly Father in solitude and prayer. His presence is inviting you into intimacy. Design your life around a daily retreat into His presence. Look into His face and feel His love. Listen to His voice and follow His instruction. Be broken by His holiness. Be mended by His grace. Be rebuked by His righteousness. Be encouraged by His wisdom. In His presence we are made whole. In His presence He provides. He provides just what we need in the moment. His presence is real time. Therefore persevere in prayer without ceasing (I Thessalonians 5:17). Be present in His presence!

REFLECTIONS

_____

_____

_____

_____

_____

_____

HEART PROBE

Though you probe my heart, though you examine me at night and test me,
you will find that I have planned no evil; my mouth has not transgressed.
Psalm 17:3

God's spirit is interested in probing our heart. He knows the heart is the source of our speech and conduct. The heart can conceal our anger or release it in Christ honoring conversation. Unreleased anger is ugly. It eventually comes out in damaging proportions. If our heart goes unexamined then we drift into a sick state of denial. We lose touch with reality and relegate others into our wrong thinking. Indeed a healthy heart keeps us honest and engaged. It is the tender touch of Jesus that reminds us to look inward. Otherwise we create a mess if we don't manage our motives and confess our sins. Our heart can be a hindrance or a conduit for Christ centered living. So how do we exercise the Spirit's examination of our heart and soul? What is necessary to make sure we come under the scrutiny of our Savior Jesus? How do we get to the heart of the matter?

A heart probe by God does not happen accidentally. It occurs intentionally. Just as we daily determine to take care of the physical dimension of our heart, so we are instructed to exercise our spiritual condition. Appointments, good or bad activities and life responsibilities can all crowd out our candid conversations with Christ. So margin for our Master is a must. We cannot spend all of our time doing the work of God while ignoring the voice of God. Good works from an unguarded heart only give an illusion of selfless service. Our works cannot resolve a conflicted heart. It is only under microscopic probing of the Holy Spirit do we see ourselves for who we are. Sometimes selfishness comes into focus. Other times timidity surfaces because we are afraid of conflict. It is in these moments of discovery that we invite in God's grace to heal our hurting heart.

Our words or the lack thereof is evidence of what dwells in our heart. Sometimes the Holy Spirit checks our heart and moves us to silence. Trust trumps the trouble we face and we exhibit longsuffering with the Lord and people. This is a heart of faith. Other times the Spirit prompts us to speak up. We are unclear of the outcomes but He gives us the courage to converse. This is a heart of boldness. Whether in silence or speech it is the Holy Spirit that governs a heart controlled by Christ. Therefore do not allow your words to get ahead of your heart. Don't speak your mind until your heart has been examined and set free by the Spirit. Sometimes a simple good night's sleep brings perspective into focus. Furthermore bear your soul before you Savior before you boldly confront.

Your heart probe may come from a variety of exercises. It may be a prescription of perpetual prayer that penetrates grace and forgiveness into your heart. It may be the treadmill of trust that builds endurance and creates within you a stronger heart of faith. Sometimes our Savior's stethoscope of conviction discovers sin that needs confession and repentance. Above all else lay your heart before the Lord. Ask others to validate the Lord's probing and promptings. Resolve by God's grace to keep short sin accounts. A Spirit probed heart produces right speech, spoken the right way. Effectiveness on behalf of our Heavenly Father hinges on a healthy heart. Therefore allow the Lord to examine it often. The Spirit's scripts are just what we need. Administer them daily!

REFLECTIONS

_____

_____

_____

_____

_____

_____

12

TRUST PERSEVERES

For the King trusts in the Lord, through the unfailing love
of the Most High he will not be shaken.
Psalm 21:7

Trust in God perseveres. It perseveres the higher it goes in responsibilities or the lower it goes in lost opportunities. Whether in the excitement of promotion or the discouragement of demotion it still trusts God. In fact the more responsibility we gain the more we need God. The more it seems we are capable, the more we realize we are incapable without Christ. Power may tempt us to lower our guard on trusting God, but just the opposite is true. The more responsibility we are entrusted with the more we are to trust the Lord. Kings and Presidents need Christ as much or more as paupers and priests. Trust is not contingent on our felt need. It is contingent on our having the ability to breathe. As long as we have breath in our lungs we desperately need the Lord. Self confidence is an obstacle to our holy confidence in Christ. He sees us through. Trust in Him perseveres.

Trust perseveres because it is buoyant in its belief in the unfailing love of God. The love of God stands secure in the face of suffering. The love of God licks the wounds of a lacerated soul. The love of God provides the grace to forgive and to forget. The love of God continues in the face of ugly odds because it is optimistic of what we can hope for in Christ. God's love draws us into intimacy with our Himself. It is when we are loved by God that we feel safe. It is when we are loved by God that we feel secure. It is when we are loved by God we feel support and encouragement. The love of God covers our sin of unbelief. It is a buttress for our belief. It is the love of the Most High that lifts us when we are at our lowest to still trust our sympathizing Savior. He is high and lifted up so He can lift us up. He looks down on us with compassion. Because He is trustworthy we trust.

No one is higher than Almighty God. He is the Most High. We have the privilege, the opportunity and the obligation to go right to the top. The Holy Spirit is God's gatekeeper. And by faith we can trust Him to intercede on our behalf. Our faith may be faltering in our confusion, but Christ clarifies. Do not give up because of the complexities of your current situation. Go the Most High to unravel the mess you find yourself. He is the decision maker. He is your maker. He knows how to guide you through this uncertain process. The Most High has the needed perspective to see you through. It is by faith that we do not completely falter. Trust Him to tell you what you need to know. Persevere.

The fruit of trust is perseverance. The lethal and high winds of adversity may attempt to uproot your faith but you will persevere. You will persevere in your –marriage though our culture gives you a pass for divorce. You will persevere in your job even though you have been passed over by someone less qualified. You will persevere as a parent because this may be your time to mature and grow up. You will persevere as a leader because God is not finished spreading your influence. You will persevere as a Christian because you trust God. By God's grace you will not be moved. Allow Him to grow your character but stand strong. Allow Him to love you through this time of transition. Trust perseveres.

REFLECTIONS

_____

_____

_____

_____

_____

_____

13

TRUST REQUIRED

*Yet you brought me out of the womb, you made me trust in you
even at my mother's breast.*
Psalm 22:9

God requires us to trust from our birth. In the beginning we are totally dependent on others. God uses doctors, nurses and midwives to navigate us out the birth canal. There is nothing we could do to gain access into this life other than wait on the warm embrace of others. Furthermore it was God's work that brought us into the world. He conceived us in our mother's womb and He brought us out of our mother's womb. There is never been a time we have not been required to trust the Lord. He knew we needed this requirement from the outset. Trust is who we are. It is part of our DNA. Our Savior stamped on our infant soul "trust in me is required". Since we took our first breathe, until we take our last breathe, we are required to trust in God. There is no getting around His requirement. He made us trust in the beginning, so we would learn to continue a life of trust in Him.

We were born desperately needy. The milk from our mother's breast sustained our life. She was our lifeline. She was the nurturer we trusted without reservation. In the same way we depend on the milk of God's word. We are babies in our belief in need of the elementary principles of the faith. The writer of Hebrews 5:12-13 says, "In fact, though by this time you ought to be teachers, you need someone to teach you the elementary truths of God's word all over again. You need milk, not solid food!" But then he goes on to say that we need more than milk for a mature faith. "Anyone who lives on milk, being still an infant, is not acquainted with the teaching about righteousness". At the genesis of our faith we were infants who sucked life from our Savior Jesus. Like a scuba diver exploring the vast unknown underwater world; He was air for our soul. We trusted Him totally as our redeemer and refuge. Trust was required then. Trust is required now.

In this life we never graduate from our Savior's school of trust. We are in Christ's classroom of trust until we graduate to heaven. It is a required course for Christ followers. He loved us as an infant and He does not cast us off in our riper years.

He was our God when we left our mother and He will be our God when we return to mother earth. Be glad that God requires trust in Him. Trust connects us to Christ. It keeps us close to Him. There is no better place to be than near the heart of God. Trust Him to love you in spite of those you distrust. Do not project your –distrust of others on the Divine.

Moreover trust in others is required for robust relationships. Do not replace trust with skepticism because of the few who have fractured your faith in people. Yes in the beginning because of relational inexperience you may have been naïve in your trust of others. But do not allow these few bruising relationships to keep you from trusting. If you trust God you can trust others. Little faith in God leads to –little faith in people. A big faith in God thinks the best of others. He can control your feelings of being controlled. Don't be defensive with your spouse or co-workers. Trust them that they are in this with you. You want them to trust you, so trust them. Trust is required for growing relationships!

REFLECTIONS

_____

_____

_____

_____

_____

_____

TRUST OVERCOMES FEAR

Even though I walk through the valley of the shadow of death, I will fear
no evil, for you are with me; your rod and your staff, they comfort me.
Psalm 23:4

Fear engages an ongoing assault on our heart and mind. If left
unchecked fear can whip our imagination up into a frenzy of anxiety. Though only
an ounce of what we fear may come to pass we tend to give it a ton of attention.
It is madness when we are overcome by fear. It may be the fear of death that
dilutes our faith. It may be the fear of failure that drives us to control. It may be
the fear of rejection that keeps us from speaking up. It may be the fear of financial ruin that refrain us from risks. It may be the fear of divorce that shatters our
dreams of a fulfilling family. It may be the fear of losing a job that becomes a self-
fulfilling prophecy. Whatever fears preoccupy our thinking we are not alone.

Jesus walks with us through our valleys. He may not deliver us out of the valley,
but He mostly certainly does not abandon us in the valley. He walks with us
through the valley of doubt. He walks with us through the valley of shame. He
walks with us through the valley of transition. He walks with us through the valley
of disease. He walks with us through the valley of the shadow of death. Our fear
many times is but a shadow of Satan's. It is not real. It seems like reality but it is
not. It is but a reflection of the evil one. So we have no need to fear because our
Heavenly Father casts His long light of love. A shadow assumes a light. Therefore
the light of Christ is there to guide us through the shadows of our soul. Death
stands next to our path of life and attempts to cast a shadow, but the light of heav-
en guides our way. We trust Jesus. Trust overcomes fear.

We trust the Lord with the known and the unknown. There may be consequences
from relational baggage that we still unpack from our past. This is fruit from foolish choices that we have to take responsibility and trust God. Good can still come
out of unwise actions, but good is gained as we regain our trust in Christ. In our
valleys we can forget our faith and be consumed by our fears, or we can slow down
and let the Lord love us through this time of loss. No amount of pain can separate

you from the love of God. Pain may be smothering your soul. But do not give up on God. Immerse yourself in the Psalms where David sometimes drowns in doubt, but by faith wisely lifts an arm to the Lord. No one suffers well alone. It is with the Almighty and the prayers of others we make it through.

So go to Christ for comfort. His tools of trust invite us. He repairs our broken - -spirit with His rod and His staff. He comforts our crushed heart with His caring touch. When we stray as curious or lost sheep He doesn't give up on us, rather He goes after us. Indeed love is not passive. It initiates contact, comfort and connection. Love helps you make sense out of a senseless situation. At the very least the Lord will bring clarity to your confusion. Saturate your soul with truth and you will flush out your fears. Trust the ones you value most with your Heavenly Father. He -values them more than you and will make sure their needs are met. Trust Him as you face your fears, whether of death or life. Trust in Christ is a bridge to His comfort. Above all else trust in the Lord overcomes fear!

REFLECTIONS

_____

_____

_____

_____

_____

_____

QUALIFICATIONS FOR CLOSENESS

Who may ascend the hill of the LORD ? Who may stand in his holy place?
He who has clean hands and a pure heart, who does not lift up his soul
to an idol or swear by what is false. He will receive blessing from
the LORD and vindication from God his Savior.   Psalm 24:3-5

Sincere worshippers of God long to be close to Christ. This is our eternal end game. This is the outcome we crave. It is closeness to Christ that places us in the proximity for Him to wipe away our tears. It is closeness to Christ that reveals our sin and leads us to repentance. It is closeness to Christ that instills the best perspective. It is closeness to Christ that calms our heart, engages our mind and sets our feet to dancing. There is no earthly substitute for the fulfillment and the feeling of significance that comes from snuggling up to our Savior. But it is not without effort on our part. Just as a teenager has to slow down long enough to be with their parents so we have to gear back and get with God. A life of chronic activity misses intimacy with the Almighty.

Furthermore closeness comes from cleanliness. We came from the dirt. We started out unclean. Dirt in our heart throws off dust in our eyes. We struggle to see God when we have not cleansed our heart. The pure in heart see God (Matthew 5:8). But the impure of heart are like blind bats fluttering around in futility. We are from the dirt in the valley and He is high a top His holy mountain. The snow capped mountain of God is pure and clean. The air is crisp and clear without the pollution of earthly emissions. So as we ascend to the Almighty by faith we ask Christ to clean us up so we can go up. We confess motives that are full of self and void of humility. We come clean over our lust and covetousness. We ask God to remove our anger and replace it with patience and kindness. We lay our lies before the Lord and ask Him to convert them to honesty and uprightness.

So we approach the holy hill of the Lord with clean hands and a pure heart. It is an outward and inward purification that we pursue. Our behavior and our beliefs both need sanitizing. One without the other and we still limp along distant from the Lord. Closeness to Christ comes when we align both our actions and our attitude. Our ways have to match our words, or no one will listen to our claim of loyalty to the Lord. It is when what we say we believe transforms the way we talk and relate to others that we draw into intimacy with Jesus. A soft spoken person who has a hard heart is still in the foot hills of faith, outside the mountain top of maturity. Pride may be masked in the moment but overtime it will lash out in anger and rejection. Therefore come clean with Christ. We would not expect a server to bring out our meal with soiled hands. Nor are we to serve our Lord with the dirt of denial under our fingernails. Clean hands and a pure heart raise us up.

God trusts those whom He holds close to His chest. He trusts them because they are near by to hear His instructions and obey His commands. Indeed hunger for His heart. Thirst for His trust. Closeness continually communes. It is not like the adult child who only comes close to home when they need something. Instead hang out often. There is intentionality into intimacy. This qualifies you for closeness to Christ. God trusts those whom He believes in. He blesses those who are close by. Therefore stay close to Christ!

REFLECTIONS

_____

_____

_____

_____

_____

_____

16

SHAMELESS HOPE

No one whose hope is in you will ever be put to shame, but they will
be put to shame who are treacherous without excuse.
Psalm 25:3

We are shameless when our hope is in our Savior Jesus Christ.

Hope in Jesus resides in a no shame zone. We have nothing to be ashamed of
when our hope is in heaven. Others may make fun of our simple faith, but they
cannot shame us. Ironically critics of faith are the ones to be ashamed. They are
without hope. Hope outside of Christ is a caricature of positive expectations.
Misplaced hope is a shame. It is a sham. It leads to deep disappointment and
disillusionment. Shame is the reward of sin. On the other hand freedom is the fruit
of hope. We have nothing to be embarrassed about when we hope in the eternal.
We have something solid to look forward to when we look to the Lord for hope and
encouragement. Hope in Jesus is never put to shame.

However hope many times is related to our hurt. It is out of our pain that hope in
Christ seems the most compelling. Our pain from suffering produces a need and
capacity for hope. Suffering enlarges the heart by creating the power to sympa-
thize. When we have lived poor we have more of a tendency to empathize with the
poor. When we or a loved one have combated disease our prayers are on the look
out for the ill. When we have seen our families ripped apart by death or divorce
we have a soft spot in our heart for a single parent and their children. It is in our
hope that we are able to extend hope to the hopeless. We can be grateful for the
occasional grief we encounter if it preserves us from hopeless hard heartedness.
Hope filled hearts are on the look out for those seeking the Lord. So it is out of
our hurt that hope comes alive for us and others.

Furthermore our hope is reserved for us in heaven. Our Heavenly Father owns our
hope. He is an owner that we never have to fear embarrassment. Our Savior's
hope will never bring shame to our situation. No rational thinking person would
say, "What a shame that Christians have forgiveness of their sins, abundant living
on earth and the hope of heaven." If anything people without hope may be jeal-

ous and ashamed of their own hopeless condition. Lastly the Lord dispenses hope liberally and indiscriminately. Jesus is not stingy with hope. He extends hope as a generous giver, gladly and cheerfully. It gives God great joy to give hope to His children. His part is to give our part is to receive.

So heaven's hope is alive and well. It is waiting for the engagement of faithful followers of Jesus. Like a secret garden accessible by faith alone we have the luscious environment of hope for our enjoyment. We can sit and smell the flowers of God's faithfulness. We can bite into the delicious juicy fruit of God's peace. We can stand without fear in the warm light of the Lord because we are full of hope. Hope lifts the veil of shame and replaces it with the face of encouraging expectations. Pessimism is replaced with optimism. Inertia is replaced with energy. Excuses are replaced with ambition. Defeat is replaced with victory. We can be extremely grateful and not ashamed that our hope is in Jesus. Hope may be lost for a season, so do not be ashamed to continually seek the Lord. Seek Him while He can be found (Isaiah 55:6). You will find hope in Him. Hope is God's way to love and encourage you and others. Hope is not ashamed

REFLECTIONS

_____

_____

_____

_____

_____

_____

17

LOVE AND TRUTH

for your love is ever before me, and I walk continually in your truth.
Psalm 26:3

Walk in truth and be lead by love. These are twins of wise living. Love is our leader and truth is our motivator. Love is our strategy and truth is our tactic. Love is our goal and truth is our inspiration. Love is our encouragement and truth is our obedience. We need both to become better followers of Jesus. We are not under the bondage of the law, but we are under the sweet constraints of grace. Love without truth can be deceived with every new form of teaching. It can be easily swayed by emotion instead of remaining stable and confident in Christ. Truth without love becomes judgmental and harsh. It can go through the right motions while resentment builds unabated. Love and truth work together so we are able to live a compelling Christian life. They bring us into balance.

This is why we look forward to the love of God as a guide for our faith. Faith trusts God to accomplish His own decrees. This is why we do not have to steal for we know God will provide for His children. This is why we do not have to get back others in revenge because God can and will handle them in His timing and in His way. This is what it means to be led by the love of God. You can trust God's love to dispense justice when appropriate and extend grace and forgiveness as needed. He sees the bigger picture and knows what is necessary to draw others closer to Christ. This is why we look ahead to the love of God. When we look to love as the leader we trust. We follow love by faith.

Secondly we walk grounded in truth. Truth governs our faith. Truth keeps us rooted in reality. It is obedience to God's truth that proves our love for Him. Truth takes us back to the adage of "What does the Almighty think I should be and do?" We walk in truth because it preserves us from sinful behavior. It is the assurance of God's promises that causes us to imitate them as well as believe. Like a pilot who depends on instruments, radar, radio and GPS (Global Positioning System) to guide him on the best path to the right destination, so we walk in truth expecting the Lord's best outcomes. Some talk of truth, but it is much better to walk in truth. Some vow to do better in the future, but their resolutions come to nothing. Avoid those who say one thing and do another.

A companion of fools suffers harm (Proverbs 13:20). Stay away from those who stray from the truth. It may be a pastor, teacher, friend or business client who handles the truth loosely. They lie even when the truth will do. These are vain people. Do not sit with them and be drawn in by their sincere charisma. Their pretentious 'pixy dust' is deceptive. However those who walk in the truth will at times tell you things you do not want to hear. They are your internist on eternal matters. So listen when they prescribe doses of truth. The medicine may go down distasteful but if applied will heal your heart. Therefore walk in truth, and walk with those who walk in truth. Love leads and truth follows. Go with God. Go to Him often and receive gladly his infinite love and insightful truth. He is both!

REFLECTIONS

_____

_____

_____

_____

_____

_____

18

CONFIDENT IN CRISIS

Though an army besiege me, my heart will not fear; though war
break out against me, even then will I be confident.
Psalm 27:3

A crisis is in the eye of the beholder. One man's crisis is another man's opportunity. One man's crisis is another man's dread. In a crisis faith either moves front and center or to the end of the line. During a moment of crisis our heart can feel overwhelmed by the perception of an encamped enemy. Fear creeps into our feelings and we begin to falter in our faith. An encamped enemy can instill as much dread as the actual battle. It is during these interim times that we sometimes fear the most. Crisis' of course come and go. A terminal patient does not linger forever. There is a beginning and an end. A financial shortfall may require layoffs and budget cuts, but at some point the hemorrhaging of cash stops. A marriage malfunction may blow up in divorce or get better by dealing in the realities of communication, love and unselfish service. Relationships develop or decay. It is in crisis mode that we reject our instinct to panic and become desperate.

Instead we trump feelings with faith. God has brought us safe thus far. He faithfully guides all who follow by faith. Fear erodes our confidence in Christ and replaces it with anger and defensiveness. We capitulate into our feeling that we have to be in control. We believe we have to take charge and corral the cause in our strength and ingenuity. However, "If God be with us, who can be against us?" (Romans 8:31). He is our light and our salvation, who shall we fear. The light of His love illumines our uncertain path. We do not have to fall prey to the tactics of the dark side and doubt Him. We can go forward by faith. There is one thing we need in the middle of a crisis. It is imperative that we dwell in the house of the Lord, that we seek Him in His temple. In the day of trouble He will keep us safe in His dwelling. He hides us in the shelter of His tabernacle and sets us high upon a rock (Psalm 27:4-5). In crisis, we have joyful confidence in Christ.

Confidence in crisis means we are collaborative and not combative. Confidence takes the high road of respect. There is no need to blame others or beat them down with verbal attacks. Persuasive people are prone to pride. They are forceful with their feelings. However people confident in Christ collaborate. Collaboration seeks out the opinion of others. There is an invitation for intellectual engagement. There is an investment in blocks of time for deep dialogue and discussion. Crisis tries to cause shortcuts, but confident and collaborative teams take the time for convergence of the best thinking to take place. A crisis needs our pride in perception to respect another's ideas. Our past experience may not be what's best for the future direction of the enterprise.

It is a confident and courageous leader who can give up control and trust the Lord and others with the process. Those who are collaborative for Christ are positioned to be more than conquerors through Christ. Where there is no confidence in Christ, there is no continuance with Christ. Overcome your fears by faith in Jesus. He is just what you need. Hold your family, job and opinions with an open hand. Trust Him and others in the process of crisis management. We can be confident in Christ in crisis. No fear by faith!

REFLECTIONS

_____

_____

_____

_____

_____

_____

VOICE OF GOD

The voice of the LORD is over the waters; the God of glory thunders,
the LORD thunders over the mighty waters.
Psalm 29:3

God's voice has not vanished. He has not lost His voice because of over use. His vocal cords are not strained but clear. God does not cough or become congested. His voice is strong and intelligible. His voice is all around us, for us to listen and be in awe. Thunder and lightening display their glory in the heavens, but they are commissioned by Christ. They are natural phenomena, but they originate from the Almighty. Thunder appears from the most high and is independent from man. It is a work of God. It is the voice of God poetically, figuratively and instructively. His voice through nature invites our awe and our attention. We hear His thunder and gaze up in both fear and amazement. His voice reminds us of His glory. It is the glory of God that thunders from heaven in the heavens.

The glory of God governs the heavens. Electricity in itself is powerless. It is ignited by Almighty God. He is the source of light, heat, cold and darkness. God is the creator and the sustainer of earth. His creation continues because He continues to create. Just as human beings are an ongoing creation of the Lord, so the earth is the Lord's ongoing creation. He resides in eternity but still engages with earth. His glory has not been gutted by scientific explanations only validated. We see God in the dark clouds and the upper water of rain, and we give Him credit for the lower water of the seas. Our Savior can be seen in the beauty of His creation. Christ can be seen in all corners of His creation. His voice is powerful and majestic. It cannot go unnoticed by any honest individual.

The power of His voice is illustrated in nature and applied in our life. His voice can be stern in discipline or tender in grace. Wise are His children who respond to both. The powerful voice of Jesus called Lazarus back from the dead, and on His death bed interceded to His Heavenly Father for forgiveness on behalf of His enemies. We do well to imitate Christ's voice of faith and compassion. Use your voice to pray for people who are dead in their sin in need of a soften heart toward their

Savior Jesus. Lift up your voice on behalf of others who have offended you and your friends. God hears your voice. He honors the voice of those who vicariously cry out on behalf of unbelievers. It may seem like you are a lone voice for the Lord, but you are not. God has His people around you.

God's voice is majestic and regal. He is enthroned above all His creation. Jehovah Jesus is our King of Kings and Lord of Lords. When He speaks we listen. His words matter most. The Holy Bible is the wisdom of His words in written form. His voice speaks through the pages of Scripture. So milk His meaning for you from His written word. Take what He tells you and obediently apply it to your life, then tell others. Those of us who hear the voice of God cannot keep quiet. He speaks in the temple of His creation and we speak in the temple of His worship - the church. The Body of Christ listens. We speak His name and He gives us strength. We speak His name and He gives us peace. Name the name of Christ for His glory and for your good. God desires to speak to us and through us. Therefore be a clean vessel for His voice to travel!

Reading #20

REFLECTIONS

_____

_____

_____

_____

_____

_____

20

SECURE NOT SHAKEN

When I felt secure, I said, "I will never be shaken." O LORD,
when you favored me, you made my mountain stand firm;
but when you hid your face, I was dismayed.
Psalm 30:6

Security rests in our Savior not our stuff. Stuff comes and goes. It is by nature insecure. But when Christ comes to dwell in our hearts He remains. Because He is secure we can be secure. But we must beware lest believe security resides anywhere else than the Lord. God has set His seal of ownership on all who believe. He has put His Spirit in our hearts guaranteeing what is to come (2 Corinthians 1:22). We have an escrow account in eternity. God is the guarantor of our eternal security. Because of this we are secure in Jesus. Our security is not based on feelings but faith. If our security depends on feeling secure we are men most miserable. Feelings of security fade in the face of trouble.

If our confidence is based on pleasant circumstances then we become careless with Christ. Our life becomes nothing more than a roller coaster of reactionary responses. If we feel good we are secure. If we feel bad we are insecure. If people like us we are secure. If they do not like us we are insecure. If we have money we are secure. If we lack money we are insecure. If we are healthy we are secure. If we are unhealthy we are insecure. If our job is certain we are secure. If our job is uncertain we are insecure. If our children are obedient we are secure. If our children are disobedient we are insecure. If things go our way we are secure. If things don't go our way we are insecure. Needless to say we eventually grow weary and wither under the whiplash of insecure living.

So do not place your security in success or failure. The fumes of success can smother your faith as fast as failure can extinguish your hope. Do not allow your material gains to become a substitute for your security in Christ. Stuff is at the top of insecurity's heap. It is the security we find in Jesus that never changes. He is our rock and our refuge. He never moves. He is not shaken. Critics could not rattle Christ with their mockery and meanness. He stood firm in His faith in His Heavenly Father. Physical abuse did not drive Him to abandon the Almighty's call on His life. It emboldened Him instead. The flames of adversity did not compromise His moral purity. Indeed suffering became His launching pad for secure and pure behavior. Hope warmed His heart with security.

Left to our own devices we are insecure people. Anytime self seeks security outside of Christ it becomes insecure. It is ironic that the search for security results in insecurity when we marginalize our Master. He is not our Lord for the last minute. He is our 'go to' God first. Secure people wrap everything about themselves around Jesus. Relationships come and go, but your relationship with Jesus remains secure. You grow smart and wiser with learned experience, but you shun intellectual snobbery and stay humbly secure in Christ. Your balance sheet balloons in net worth, but you keep your ego from inflating by remaining secure in Christ alone. Generous givers are secure. Insecurity arises when we add something to our faith in Christ. Therefore be secure in your fidelity of faith. You are secure because your security is eternal. Shun earthly securities and embrace heavens'. Faith needs no help. Above all else the faithful are secure not shaken!

REFLECTIONS

_____

_____

_____

_____

_____

_____

21

PERSONAL GOD

But I trust in your, O Lord; I say, 'You are my God'.
Psalm 31:14

God is accessible and personal to those who call on His name by faith. He is not an aloof Almighty, but an engaging One. God governs the universe and He takes time for those who come to Him. Trust in Him is a ticket to a personal relationship with Providence. Trust is a bridge of belief that spans the canyon of Christ-less concern. It is when we trust Him that we are positioned to know Him. Relationship without trust is incapable of intimacy and the feeling of closeness. This is why we place our faith in Him and not in our faith. Our faith is undependable, but our God is ever dependable. We stay steadfast in our faith in God even in the face of suffering, temptation and dire circumstances. He is still our God that can be trusted in our times of trouble. Our hope in God is so strong that we do not cease to call upon His name in our sorrow. When we know Him we trust Him.

Adversity and challenges great or small compete with out trust in God. When it seems like our brand of Christianity is not working we are tempted to give up. We want to re-brand God to fit our shallow beliefs. Because He is personal we expect Him to bend toward our immature behavior. Indeed, giving up can be good if it is giving up on our self solutions. But we cannot give up on God. Christians will let us down, but not Jesus. Christ's care is personal and persevering. He is not going anywhere. Our anger may cause us to retreat from the tender touch of our Lord, but He patiently waits for us to come back to our senses and come back to Him. Don't project your dysfunctions on your personal relationship with Jesus. Instead ask Him to make you a reflection of His grace, mercy, forgiveness, peace and holiness. Get personal with 'your God'. You can laugh with the Lord and cry with Christ. You take on the attributes of those for whom we are personal.

He is 'our God' in the sense that He owns us. We do not own the Almighty. Our actions sometimes dictate to God. We make decisions and then ask Him to bless our mess. Or we don't make decisions and we ask Him to bless our irresponsibility. Either way we sometimes try to manage up our Master. This is not healthy. This doesn't work. Our role is not to change God and others so our lives will be better. Our role is to surrender to our Savior Jesus and ask Him to change us. We are in personal relationship with Christ because we need to reflect His ownership on our lives. He is 'our God' in the same way that a person is our mayor, governor or president. We are under their authority. We submit to the laws of the land for the sake of the whole. We submit to God because He is our ultimate authority. Our rights are relegated to what God says is right.

Therefore avoid mistrust and embrace trust in the Lord. Doubt leads to death and trust leads to life. God is personal and trustworthy. Our personal prayers are directly to Him. When you do not know what to pray; ask Him to align your heart with His. Then your desires become His desires. This is the best outcome of our personal prayers. Intimacy with the Almighty leads to alignment with the Almighty. God gives us easy access so we can understand and apply His principles. He is personal for His purposes. So do not shun seeking out your Savior. He can be trusted. He is your God for His glory!

REFLECTIONS

_____

_____

_____

_____

_____

_____

22

BLESSINGS OF FORGIVENESS

Blessed is he whose transgressions are forgiven, whose sins are covered.
Psalm 32:1

Forgiveness is full of blessings. The blessing of guilt's removal is a fruit of forgiveness. The peace of being in a right relationship with God and people is facilitated by forgiveness. The freedom to follow God's will, passionately and unashamedly, is fueled by daily forgiveness. Forgiveness frees the soul and enlightens the mind. It is a state of experiencing God's grace and mercy. Forgiveness off loads laziness and replaces it with diligence. Forgiveness erases lust and writes in love. Forgiveness takes away the stain of selfishness and dyes it with service. The blessings of forgiveness are bold and belittle sin. Like the Sermon on the Mount, there is a mountain of blessings that come to the obedient.

Jesus forgives the lawbreaker not the law keeper. Foolish and naïve is the man or woman who thinks they can continually keep the law without the pardon of God's grace. Forgiveness is a daily requirement for those who want to keep short accounts with their Savior, family and friends. It is when we try to justify our bad attitudes and behaviors without repenting that we get into a crazy cycle of self-sufficiency. Knowing and acknowledging the need to do something does not free us from sin. We may kid ourselves, but discerning people know if we daily do business with God or just go through the motions of religious activity. Unless we repent of our sin from a contrite heart, there is no remission. The forerunner of Jesus, John the Baptist, taught this (Luke 3:3). Jesus gave His life so He could give us life. Jesus sweat blood so we could have sweet forgiveness.

The Bible describes a trinity of sin for the un-forgiven. In our own strength our disobedience is labeled as transgression, sin and iniquity. But the Trinity in heaven annihilates the trinity of sin. The Holy Spirit convicts us of sin and draws us into the love of our Heavenly Father. His love leads us to Jesus who gave His life on the cross to pay the penalty for our sin. We confess to Christ our need for His gracious forgiveness. In Christ we are free. We are free from guilt and free from guile. God's

Spirit uncovers our sin, cleanses it with our confession and then covers it with grace. If we conceal our sin we will not prosper (Proverbs 28:13). Mercy comes to the man who confesses. Miserable is the man who conceals. Come clean with Christ and His grace will be your residue.

Furthermore be a blessing by forgiving the un-forgiven. We are forgiven by God so that we can forgive. Extend forgiveness to those who do not deserve your forgiveness. This is grace. This is what Jesus would do and what you would want if you were in their same situation. Unconditional forgiveness is freeing. Indeed, one reason you forgive others is for your own sake. Otherwise, unforgiving relation-ships cause a root of bitterness to go deep into your heart and rob you of joy. Avoid withholding forgiveness to hurt others. Instead, you will get hurt. Let go and give to God your unfair friend, insensitive supervisor, proud parent, uncaring spouse or selfish child. Pray for them to be healed and you will be healed. Forgiveness does this. It heals the soul with eternities' elixir.

REFLECTIONS

_____

_____

_____

_____

_____

_____

23

DELIVERANCE FROM FEAR

I sought the Lord, and he answered me; he delivered me from all my fears.
Psalm 34:4

Prayer positions us to receive the peace of God. It is when we seek Him that we see Him. It is when we see Him that we are secure. As we travel across the choppy sea of life circumstances, we can become dizzy and fearful if we look down at the water of wonder. But if we keep our eyes fixed ahead on a stable object, we remain secure and feel safe. Jesus is our immovable object of belief. He is our secure Savior who is there for us when fear assaults our attitude and threatens to highjack our heart. When we seek His face He reciprocates by flooding our countenance with His peace. He replaces our furrowed brow of fear with a calm face of faith. He gives the righteous a radiant face that is never to be covered with shame. The Lord hears our prayers by extending His peaceful presence.

No one has ever been sorry for seeking the Lord. It takes time and effort but it is your best investment. Process your problems with prayer and you will be the most productive. We cannot come to the best solutions in our own strength. One dimensional problem solving only leads to average results at best. Why be satisfied with a perspective limited to your experiences, intelligence and giftedness? It is seeking the Lord that unlocks a treasure trove of truth that leads us down possibilities we would never imagine in our own head. The fruit that comes from replacing fear with faith is unlimited. We can rest assured as the Almighty leads us down a new path. This is what may happen in the process of seeking your Savior. He delights in determining a better way for you.

This next season of your life is the Lord's reward for your faithfulness all these years. You have sought Him unashamedly and obediently. Money has not been your motive. Pride has not prodded you. Fame has not been your forte. You have sought Him with your unselfish service. You have sought Him with your humble obedience. You have sought Him by ministering to the needs of others. Because of your faithfulness to seek Him He has grown your faith and marginalized your fears. Therefore see this next season as an extension of His blessings. There is no need to fear because God is near those who seek Him. There is no safer and secure place to be than in the process of seeking Him.

Moreover, God expects to hear from you before you can expect to hear from Him. If you restrain prayer; He may refrain grace and mercy. The more you think upon the Lord, and less you think of yourself, the better off you become. Seek Him, lose yourself and you will discover the best way. Furthermore, there is no need to fear your next transition as your Heavenly Father has your hand and He is guiding you. There is no need to fear the cessation of this phase of your career as He is in control. There is no need to fear the breaking off of a relationship as He is in the business of mending broken hearts. There is no need to fear your family being provided for as God is your provider. Seek Him and He will deliver you from your fears. Seek Him and you will be secure in Him. Seek Him before, during and after trouble comes. Then seeking the Lord becomes second nature to your soul. Then fear fails its' mission. Indeed, seeking Him fossilizes your fears!

REFLECTIONS

_____

_____

_____

_____

_____

_____

24

PASSIONATE PRAYER

They repay me evil for good and leave my soul forlorn.
Yet when they were ill, I put on sackcloth and humbled myself with fasting.
When my prayers returned to me unanswered, I went about mourning as
though for my friend or brother. I bowed my head in grief as
though weeping for my mother.   Psalm 35:12-14

There is a passionate prayer for our enemies. It rests in the recesses of our righteous soul. It is counter intuitive in our aggressive age of revenge and resentment. But it is intuitive for those who intercede indiscriminately to the Almighty on behalf of all people. As followers of Jesus, we do not have the right to only pray for those who love and support us. We are also called to crash the gates of heaven on behalf of those who bother us. People who do not pursue Christ, but who pursue us with malicious intent are intended to be on our prayer list. Our natural man wants to ignore those who ignore us and write them off, but Christ commands us to inscribe their names on our hearts for prayer. And it is not an obligatory prayer that we get out of the way once and then move on. It is a persistent and passionate prayer for our enemies that Christ expects.

Jesus described well our attitude toward our enemies, "You have heard that it was said, 'Love your neighbor and hate your enemy.' But I tell you: Love your enemies and pray for those who persecute you..." (Matthew 5:43-44). Your enemy can be anyone who is against you and/or against God. You feel a persistent push back from their personality. You have felt hostility towards each other and even malicious intent. You may have been harmed by them financially. Regardless of the degree of enmity, there is a relational disconnect and distrust. An enemy is not a favorite person of yours and you do not enjoy their company. It may be your parent who seems to have zero interest in your affairs. They only contact you when they need something. It may be a spouse who has invested layers of hurt into your relationship over the years and you can hardly stand to look at them. It may be a friend who has betrayed you. It may be a plaintiff in a lawsuit.

Regardless of whom we envision as our enemies we are to pray for them and love them. Our prayers are to be full of passion and pleading on their behalf. We bombard the throne of grace asking God to pour out His mercy on their behalf. They may be blinded by unbelief and groping around life in graceless confusion. Our enemies need enlightenment from our eternal Savior, Jesus. We were once enemies of the cross outside of Christ's care. We acted like we had it all together, when in reality we were poor and wretched souls lost in our sins. It is as through our fasting and prayers for those who are in the bondage of unbelief that God may choose to set them free. Passionate prayer persists.

Prayer is never in vain. If the one being prayed for is not blessed, certainly it blesses the one who intercedes on their behalf. Our prayer for our enemies changes us. It softens our hearts and speech with sympathy. It allows us to model our prayers after our master Jesus when He prayed, 'Father, forgive them, for they know not what they are doing' (Luke 23:34). Passionate prayer for our enemies is as much about us, as them. It changes us both!

REFLECTIONS

25

SELF-FLATTERY

There is no fear of God before his eyes. For in his own eyes
he flatters himself too much to detect or hate his sin.
Psalm 36:1b-2

Self-flattery is foolish. It has no fear of God. Self-flattery follows a false faith that is forged out of convenience not commitment. Self-flattery sees itself as the center of attention instead of Almighty God. It is enamored with itself. It defines and executes its own agenda. It is soft on sin. However, God-fearers see their sin and flee from its presence. It is not invited into their circle of influence. Furthermore, a person who flatters themselves does not have a proper view of God or respect for Him. Respect for God flows from fear of God. But instead self-flattery, it demands respect. There is a notion that they need to know that others hold the same high opinion of themselves as they do.

Self-flattery heaps on itself praise in substitute for penance. This is dangerous and absurd. Even the silliest bird does not set a trap for itself. To smooth over one's conduct, or to sooth it's conscience may set us up for failure. We can justify anything, but we had better be ready to suffer the consequences. There is a limit to our self-congratulation, eventually God and others grow impatient with its obnoxious ways. Our inability to own up to our actions, or lack thereof, lowers our standing with God and man. The opposite occurs with self-flattery. It loses respect instead of gaining respect. It grows discontent instead of being content. It feels worse instead of feeling better. Self-flattery fails.

There are many forms of self-flattery. When we think we are smarter than God, but we ignore the principles laid out in His word, the Bible, we flatter ourselves. When we think we have hope in heaven, but we act like hell, we flatter ourselves. When we live for today, like death is a million miles away, we flatter ourselves. When we treat others with contempt, and then expect them to follow our ways, we flatter ourselves. When we say we trust in the Lord, but then we borrow money and presume on the future, we flatter ourselves. Self-flattery longs for approval but it is denied from those who really matter. There is a better way. The better way rises above self-flattery's deception. It needs awakening from its slumber like the church Jesus spoke about (Revelation 3:17).

The road away from self-flattery is self-denial. Self-denial refrains from flattery. It is determined to know God. It is sensitive to sin and loves the Lord. The fear of God is in the forefront of those who deny themselves for the cause of Christ. Self-denial keeps God in holy awe and self away from unhealthy admiration. It makes much of God and little of self. When we see God, we admire Him and cease to flatter ourselves. Knowing God allows us to really know ourselves and discern between the two. The wisdom of God instructs us to place proper weight on what God wants verses what we want. Self-denial sends us into a whole other mindset, away from self-flattery. Its focus is being who God wants you to be and doing what God wants you to do. Self-denial serves others and defers to what they value. It thinks more highly of God and His children. Self-denial replaces self flattery with faith in God. Faith in God frees us to be secure in Him. Our identity is in Christ. We do not have to impress others or ourselves. He is all that matters. Replace self-flattery with faith in God. Faith in Him energizes an eternal self-esteem!

REFLECTIONS

_____

_____

_____

_____

_____

_____

26

ENJOY GREAT PEACE

But the meek will inherit the land and enjoy great peace.
Psalm 37:11

Meekness is a bridge to blessing. It is an attitude God honors with the enjoyment of His great peace. Meekness meanders and moves in and out of the halls of heaven. It sets us up to be served by our Savior. Meekness is the manner by which our Master can move us forward in His will. Our meekness transports us toward absolute surrender and obedience to God. It is the meek who tend to trust God. It is the meek who most want to faithfully follow Jesus. Indeed, meekness is most like Jesus. Jesus said of Himself, "I am meek..." (Matthew 11:29, KJV). It is here with meek Jesus that we find rest for our souls. However, meek does not mean we are weak; on the contrary we are strong in our Savior.

Meekness is a conduit for what Christ has for us. He has an inheritance for His children. What is His is ours. He owns the land and all that is within its expanse. We see His quiet white clouds cover the mountain tops like soft sheets. As the sun rises its warmth pulls back the submissive sheets of cloud cover and introduces us to the day. He has given us His earth for our great enjoyment. It is on the side of the green mountain of His creation that we sit quietly and contemplate on Christ. His peace prods our pride to be still and know Him. He hushes our hurried spirit to be silent before Providence. A silent tongue many times exhibits a wise head and a holy heart. We have His earth to enjoy now and to inherit in eternity. The meek understand this priceless privilege. They enjoy great peace.

Even as we suffer, we topple over tribulations with trust in Jesus while we rest in His great peace. Christ's consolations carry us along the way. His peace is a platform for His faithfulness to perform. Like an engaging drama on stage or in film, we wait until the end for the plot to unfold. If we jump to conclusions or draw premature assumptions, we may get caught up in bad beliefs or false fears. So life is a stage where God's great drama plays out. We are not to fret over what seems fearful or a forgone conclusion. God's plot is still unfolding by faith. His will is being revealed. His cast of characters is still in development. While His plot thickens, we trust. Until the end, enjoy His great peace.

Lastly, we may not have an abundance of stuff, but we have great peace. It is better to do stuff with our Savior than to have stuff without Him. He is our wisdom when we face complex circumstances. He is who we cling to in crisis. We silence our murmuring so we can be silent before Him. It is in silence before our Savior that His great peace saturates our soul. It engulfs our edginess with eternal assurance. There may be things on earth that we seem deprived of from their enjoyment aspects. But, there is coming a day where this accursed earth is no more and we will enjoy the benefits of His new earth without sin, sickness or sorrow. We will inherit the land of our Lord. In the meantime, go to God for His great peace. Like a river of love it attends to our soul with soothing security and peace. Enjoy God's great peace in Christ. Fret not, but have faith in Him. He seeks the meek!

REFLECTIONS

_____

_____

_____

_____

_____

_____

27

WAIT FOR GOD'S ANSWER

I wait for you, O Lord; you will answer, O Lord my God.
Psalm 38:15

God's answer is not always immediate. Our Heavenly Father may not be forthcoming in His answer to prayer. We wait in our pain and there seems to be no relief. We wait in our confusion and our circumstances seem to become more complicated. We wait for wisdom on how to harness our child's energy for God and we find ourselves wanting. Their rebellion seems to compound as they distance themselves from Christ. We wait in wonder of what we need to do at work. Indeed answers from the Almighty may be absent for now, but the faithful wait. We wait for God's answer because He is the source of our sanity and our security. His goal is to give us everything we need in His timing and in His way. He is not without compassion. He cares immensely to answer our prayers and give creative solutions to our questions. Pray to Him.

We commit ourselves to Christ because we know He judges righteously. He can be trusted. He is not withholding His answer for His pleasure. In fact He may have already answered and we have avoided hearing Him. Our activity can be an enemy to hearing God. You may need to slow down and stop trying to fix the faults of others. Instead slow down and be with your Savior. Seek His face and fear Him. Seek the Lord and love Him. It is in the quantity time of being with Jesus that we know how to invest quality time in doing for Jesus. His answers may not come instantly but they come over time. They come when we are ready to listen to His wisdom and apply it to our life. God doesn't speak freely to those He can't trust. But to the trustworthy He pours out His truth. Those who steward truth well are candidates to receive more insight into God's ways.

Our patience allows God to possess our soul. Hope in the Almighty's intervention and the power of prayer are what bring peace to a soul plagued by pain. It is in our adversity that the voice of the Almighty is near and clear. We just need to listen, really listen. The earwax of anger may be blocking the hearing canals of our heart.

The water of worry may stop up our souls capacity to hear Christ. The pain that racks our body may be distracting us from discerning the Lord's instruction. Whatever may be blocking our communication with Christ we need to give over to Him. We can trust Him and then listen to Him.

Do not settle for anything less than the Almighty's answer. Look for the Lord's leading in His word and among godly counsel. You will find the richest solace in waiting for His wisdom. Why settle for the scraps of a quick solution when you can have the gold of God's solid strategy? Take your team and/or family through a process of discovering God's game plan. It takes more time and trust, but it bears the fruit of God's best. Christ's answer many times is compelling and creative. Rest in the refuge of His reference. Do not allow your soul be tossed back and forth by the anxiety of not having an answer. Use this time of waiting to grow in your understanding of God. His answer is way worth the wait. Don't run ahead impatiently. He works while we wait. He expands our faith while we wait. Listen intently, discern and obey. Obedience unleashes answers. Obedience leads to opportunities. Stay faithful and patient. The Almighty will answer!

REFLECTIONS

_____

_____

_____

_____

_____

_____

28

LIFE IS SHORT

Show me, O LORD, my life's end and the number of my days; let me know
how fleeting is my life. You have made my days a mere handbreadth;
the span of my years is as nothing before you. Each man's life is but a breath.
Selah.

Sometimes we don't know what we know. We know God loves us, but we struggle with feeling loved by our Heavenly Father. We know God can be trusted, but our faith becomes fragile under the fire of financial pressures. We know God is all-wise, but we forget this and go to Him only as the last resort for instruction and discernment. Indeed we know we will die soon relative to eternity, yet we sometimes get sucked into just living in a temporal trap with no thought of tomorrow. It is very fit we ask of God that He would make us know the things that we do know.

Even heroes of the faith stumbled at staying focused on the brevity of life. David, who pursued God with passion, asks the Lord to let him know how fleeting his life looked. He needed to know what he already knew. We need to know what we already know. We forget when we get caught up in the moment and then we wonder why Christ can't use us to His fullest. So ask the Lord to remind you that there is no promise of tomorrow (James 4:13-15). Our life is the smallest of measurements. It is a handbreadth in length. Life extends from our stubby thumb of total trust at birth to our short pinky of prayer to God at death. There is not a lot in between. On average a little over a decade and a half represented by each finger on one hand. In God's big scheme of things our life is like a raindrop in the ocean or a grain of sand on the beach. It is short.

Life reminds us along the way of its temporal make up. Funerals remind us that 'death' daily escorts individuals into eternity. Each one of us, unless Jesus returns first, will be the center of attention at an all black attire event. What will those who knew you the best say at your eulogy? Will the minister be able to say you carried on a love relationship with Christ? Will your spouse say you loved unconditionally? Will your children weep because they miss your laugh and your instructing them in the ways of God, in word but mostly in deed? Will your friends feel a void because of your generous investment in their life? Writing your obituary engages you with the end.

So the Lord expects us to live with the end in mind. It is what we invest in eternity that matters in the end. People and God's word are eternal. They are worthy of our investment of time and money. Our age is irrelevant when compared to the age of the earth and the everlasting existence of our Heavenly Father. Live for the Lord of the ages. The application of His purposes makes the most sense out of your short life. Life is short and eternity is forever. Therefore live this life for your everlasting Lord!

REFLECTIONS

_____

_____

_____

_____

_____

_____

29

DISTRUST THE PROUD

Blessed is the man who makes the Lord his trust, who does not look
to the proud, to those who turn aside to false gods.

Psalm 40:4

The proud are not trustworthy. They do not trust and they cannot be trusted. They are self contained in their on little controlling world. Their motives are suspect. It is all about their agenda and their priorities. There is a sense of urgency around what they deem as important. It engulfs their environments. They only have regard to others, as they are able to use them in accomplishing their ends. The proud are bad news. They are divisive and rude. Their opinion reins supreme and they make you feel inferior if you attempt to disagree with their proud persuasion. They presume to know the facts as they define the facts. They may give lip service to the Lord, but their trust is in themselves. They even invoke the Lord's name, but only in vain.

So stay away from the influence of the proud lest you become like them. Keep your distance from those whose heart is hollow of humility. Yes the proud may be attractive because of their accomplishments. But even the devil can get things done. We do not worship at the throne of worldly success and business genius that proudly takes the credit. Proud people with high net worth are not the bottom line of which we embrace as our examples of how to live life. Models worth following are those who are quick to give God the glory for their family and work successes. They bow humbly before God's throne of grace and offer Him the fruits of their labor by faith. Trust the humble in heart and keep an eye on those who press the flesh of pride.

Be especially weary of those who portray an air of humility but mask a proud heart underneath. This may be the most hideous sin because it is unseen to the naïve and naked eye. False humility wants you to believe what is not true. False humility smiles when it is not really happy. False humility serves but only out of fear of the object of its service. False humility acts nice but all the while resentment is building that one day will erupt in horrid hatred. False humility is pride in disguise.

It is the worst kind of pride because you don't see it coming. So ask God for discernment. Avoid those who act righteous, who are only compliant for fear of rejection.

Lastly deal daily with pride in your own heart and mind. Trust in God means you do not trust in yourself. It is all about Him and His game plan. Success makes you think you are something. Indeed run from taking credit for results. Make sure to involve others in decision-making. It is not your way or the highway. Others have excellent ideas. Humbly listen to the great thoughts of thinking people. Help people think, but do not do their thinking for them. God's way is the best way. Tap into His truth. Trust Him with people and circumstances. Wait patiently on the Lord. His way will prevail by prayer and patience. The humble hone in on heaven's agenda. They trust. Distrust the proud but trust the humble. Jesus did. We trust Him as His humble followers!

REFLECTIONS

_____

_____

_____

_____

_____

_____

30

INTEGRITY'S STABILITY

In my integrity you uphold me and set me in your presence forever.
Psalm 41:12

Integrity is a stabilizing force in our life. It comes from God and it is meant for God. Integrity is based on the strong moral principles of our Master Jesus. It is the foundation of what makes our faith compelling and attractive. Lives built on this strong slab of faith with Christ as the chief cornerstone (Ephesians 2:20) have integrity. Integrity is the missing ingredient from anemic believers in the Almighty. If our 'walk does not match our talk' we have no solid standing with our Savior, or people we are seeking to influence and lead. It is your integrity that invites good and honest people to stay engaged in the enterprise you are attempting to build. It is your integrity that compels your children to come to you for counsel and advice. Integrity opens doors for your influence to flourish. It is consistent honesty. It provides moral authority.

Maintaining integrity is not always easy. Sometimes it cost us something. Maintaining your integrity may mean walking away from a relationship that reeks with inconsistencies. This person is leading you away from the Lord instead of toward Him. Your integrity may be in question because of your involvement with a questionable character. Stay above reproach in your relationships. Above all else, protect your integrity. It is your creditability as a Christ follower. As you engage in financial dealings stay away from gray areas. Gray areas can turn into a black hole of financial irresponsibility. They can drown you in the red ink of debt. Be honest about money.

Sin seeks to sink our integrity. It wants to torpedo our testimony with temptation's allure. Indeed, we are all candidates for sin without the character of Christ consuming us. It is the Holy Spirit that pricks our consciences early so we don't continue down a path of destruction. Our integrity places us in a strong and stable position to discern sin and stand against its assault. Our innocence is the result of God's upholding. When others are ensnared by sin it strikes fear into followers of Jesus. This is our fate of where we go, but for God's grace. Since we are under our Savior's surveillance we can insist on being an example of integrity. Integrity matters.

It matters because it positions us to be in the presence of God. This is the reward of walking in integrity. The Lord walks lock step with His honest and humble worshippers. His presence propels us to praise and obey Him. We are in His presence forever. Our experience in His presence remains unbroken from this life until the next. It is in His presence that we bring glory to God. Our awareness and acknowledgement of the Almighty ushers others into His presence. It is our integrity that allows us to invite others into experiencing God. Therefore, steward your integrity well. It is God's instrument of righteousness reserved for His glory. Integrity stabilizes!

REFLECTIONS

_____

_____

_____

_____

_____

_____

31

GUIDING LIGHT

*Send forth your light and your truth, let them guide me;
let them bring me to your holy mountain, to the place where you dwell.*
Psalm 43:3

God is our guiding light. The Holy Spirit is our halogen headlight from heaven. Without the Lord's guiding light we are lost. At just the right time the beautiful beams of His light break through our clouds of uncertainty. He is the Master at making sure we can see the next step in His will. We can trust Him with this sequence of steps that mark His ways. He does not want us to be preoccupied or overwhelmed with the understanding of His far away will. He understands that contentment lies in abiding with Christ in the immediate and hoping for His best in the future. Therefore, hold the Lord's lantern of truth over your next step and you will see clearly.

Furthermore, there is a direct connection between truth and light. The more the truth we learn and apply the greater the capacity for illumination. Ignorance keeps us in the dark. Sin locks us up in the ill lit light of solitude and confinement. There is little light in the Lord's ways where truth has been abandoned. As the sun sends forth its radiant rays, all nature gains life. So as the Lord sends forth the light of His love, mercy and holiness, His people grow in grace. Indeed, truth illuminates the light of the Lord with increased watts of wisdom. Our Savior Jesus is the bright star we follow. He is our guiding light when the going gets rough. By faith follow His light.

Sin may have suckered you into some dark place. You are afraid and unsure of what to do next. It may cost you an opportunity or a friendship, but it is time to leave the cold and clammy circumstance that withholds heaven's light. Trust God by repenting of the behavior that has you bound up on the inside. The reason you cannot see clearly what to do next may be due to the cloud of compromise hovering over your heart. Satan extends confusion. Christ gives clarity. Moreover, leave the dark days of your past behind you. Do not allow guilt to govern your decisions. The sins of your youth are forgiven. God has a productive path before you. His truth and light is your guide. The Holy Spirit has been here before. Trust Him with the unseen and the seen.

Lastly, lead others into the truth and the light of the Lord. Take a risk and organize a Bible study over lunch at work. Take your team through a discovery process of timeless principles that make successful people and great companies. Do not be shy with your Savior. He hung naked in public display on the cross to pay for our sin. The least we can do is carry the torch of truth on His behalf. He has you in a place of influence at work and home to be a light of love, acceptance and accountability. Do not hide your light under a rock of regret. Pray before meals and meetings. Ask others how you can pray for them. Very few turn down prayer. Stay a student of truth and then teach others. Walk in the light of the Lord and then lead others to join you. God is our guiding light!

REFLECTIONS

_____

_____

_____

_____

_____

_____

32

THROUGH GOD

Through you we push back our enemies;
through your name we trample our foes.
Psalm 44:5

Through God we get things done. It is not our superior intellect that accomplishes great things; rather it is His wisdom and 'know how'. It is not our outstanding leadership that everything depends; rather it's the leadership of the Holy Spirit that gets us to where we need to go. It is not our financial prowess that produces the biggest results, rather it's the riches of the Lord's resources that extend into eternity. Through God is how we need to govern our lives. Our 'gut' instinct will get us into trouble if it is not validated through Christ's confirmation. "Not by might nor by power, but by my Spirit,' says the LORD Almighty" (Zechariah 4:6). He gets us through dire circumstances in spite of ourselves.

Through God is how you get through divorce. Through God is how you get through serving time in prison. Through God is how you get through teenagers. Through God is how you get through transitions. Through God is how you get through traumatic experiences. Through God is how you get through a financial quagmire. Through God is how you get through relational reconciliation. It is through God that we are able to see things through. In our own strength and power we struggle to persevere. It is through Him that we receive heaven's 'back up' support and stamina.

In union and communion with Christ we can work wonders. He never ceases to amaze us because the Almighty is authentically amazing. There is nothing about God that is not good and worth emulating. It is through the engrafting of His character into our character that we pay Him the greatest compliment. Indeed it is in and through the Lord's shaping of our soul that we become more sensitive to His Spirit. It is only as we cooperate with Christ that we can experience Him working through us. Do not underestimate how God can work through you. He can take the weakest of His saints and make them equal to any task. Paul discovered the strength of his Savior at his weakest points, "That is why, for Christ's sake, I delight in weaknesses, in insults, in hardships, in persecutions, in difficulties. For when I am weak, then I am strong" (2Corinthians 12:10).

Therefore, do things through God and you will not regret the results. His results matter most. His results last. The Lord's results are lasting because they are aligned with His sovereign plan. No on can thwart what God can do through a trusting follower. It is by faith that He uses you to accomplish His will though others may be more capable. A broken and submissive follower of Jesus with average ability is exceedingly superior to a self-reliant believer with greater skills and potential. Furthermore, stay focused on what your Heavenly Father can do through you, not what you can do for Him. He doesn't need us, but we desperately need Him. It is utter dependence on Christ that positions us to be a vessel of love, wisdom and encouragement. Above all else, stay connected with Christ in humble prayer and adoration. Prostrate your soul before His throne of grace and watch Him do radical works through you for His glory. Lasting success is found through God alone!

REFLECTIONS

_____

_____

_____

_____

_____

_____

33

ENTHRALLED BY BEAUTY

The king is enthralled by your beauty; honor Him, for he is your Lord.
Psalm 45:11

Your beauty enthralls God. It is first the beauty of your belief in Christ that attracts you to almighty God. When you embrace His Son as your salvation you gain the absolute approval and blessing from your Heavenly Father. The beauty of your belief is in the eye of the beholder, God. There is nothing more you can do to gain God's acceptance than to accept His son Jesus. This makes you beautiful to Him. No longer are you dressed in the deception of sinful rags. When you were 'dressed down' by Deity you confessed belief. Now you are 'dressed up' in a righteous royal robe by faith in Christ. Your breath taking beauty of belief in Him compels Christ to come to you. Unfeigned faith attracts Jesus.

Your internal attractiveness makes your external appearance and attitude inviting. God starts by beautifying the heart and then He brings the body into His submission. A body can be beautiful but without a clean heart it is not attractive to Christ or His committed followers. This is why the pretty and the handsome that love Jesus have a stewardship to point people beyond themselves to God. He has given you a platform of attractiveness for His glory. People are attracted to you because of Him. Let them know there is a greater purpose beyond your pretty persona. There is a much higher good than your good looks. Indeed, outward beauty fades while inward beauty grows more attractive. You want to grow old with someone who embraces this beautiful truth. Otherwise beauty betrays.

Furthermore, dads have the opportunity and responsibility to tell their daughters they are beautiful. Look them in the eyes as the Lord's representative and express to them the blessing of their beauty. Tell them how you love their smile and the joy it brings to your heart. Describe to them the beauty of their pure eyes and how it is a reflection of their clean heart. Communicate to them daily with spoken and written words how proud you are of them and how attractive they are to the Lord. Use respectful words and courteous acts to affirm their sensitive hearts. Daughters desperately need their dad's approval.

Lastly, let the Lord love on you in the beauty of His holiness. Just as the church is the Bride of Christ, so have we entered into an individual and intimate relationship with Him. Beauty goes both ways. Jesus is beautiful to His believers. We adore Him. We were first attracted to Almighty God because of His consistent character. He is totally trustworthy and true. Christ brings us contentment. God is a satisfying sight for seeking eyes. Sin produces sore eyes. Our Savior sooths them. Jesus is beautiful because His grace gushes forth to free us from our immature ways.

The Almighty is attractive because He is without end. Indeed, we are beautiful to God and He is beautiful to us. There is a mutual attractiveness that mirrors marriage at its best. Therefore, stay engaged with God. See yourself as He sees you: beautiful and accepted. See Him as He is: lofty and lovely. Worship Him in the beauty of His holiness. Allow Him to love on you with an everlasting love. Beauty attracts beauty. Without Christ we are beastly. In Christ we are beautiful. Rest in and enjoy your everlasting beauty!

REFLECTIONS

_____

_____

_____

_____

_____

_____

34

GOD REIGNS

God reigns over the nations; God is seated on his holy throne.
Psalm 47:8

God reigns over the entire earth. He is not just the God of the east or the God of the west. He is the God of the north, south, east and west. The long arm of the Lord reigns over everyone. The sun never sets on the omnipresent shadow of our Savior Jesus. Indeed, He is the greatest in power, high and lofty in dominion, extremely eminent in wisdom and elevated in excellence of glory. Our God reigns. Our God reigns. He reigns in war. He reigns in peace. He reigns in crisis. He reigns in calm. He reigns in economic catastrophe. He reigns in economic prosperity. Our God reigns. He reigns over evil. He reigns over good. He reigns over nations. He reigns over individuals. Our God reigns.

Moreover, He reigns from His holy throne. His is not a throne soiled with corruption and self-serving scenarios. His throne is full of grace and truth. His throne is marked and defined by holiness. It is a throne that has never been stained with sin, corrupted by cover up or defiled by injustice. God is seated on His holy throne. He never sits dismayed or in a dilemma. God does not ring His hands in worry. He sits in serenity for He knows His own power, and He sees that His purposes will not miscarry. He sits on a throne that dispenses truth and wisdom. Therefore, approach His holy throne boldly but reverently.

Furthermore, God reigns over the human heart. It is here that we can submit to or spurn the Almighty's authority. We are wise to jettison the latter. It is in submission to our reigning King Jesus that we come to know His will for our lives. Obedience leads to opportunity. Because our God reigns, He can be trusted. His rules are for our good pleasure. Christ is not a cosmic killjoy. His rules are inviting when we are in right relationship with our reigning King. It is when we resist Him that we foolishly push back from His gracious guidelines. Therefore, love Him and you will love to follow His statutes. Indeed, our God reigns in love and holiness. It is easy to follow an unconditional lover. He reigns lovingly.

Therefore, we have reason to celebrate Christ's reign. His kingship brings praise to our lips. Our Lord reigns. Halleluiah! We have no real reason to worry and to stress out because our God reigns. We can put the kibosh on our complaining and murmuring because our God reigns. We can rest in a peaceful sleep at night, and not toss and turn in distrust because our God reigns. We can let go of control and not be controlled because our God reigns. We can give Him our grief, sorrow, and sin because our God reigns.

Our God reigns for the purpose of His glory and His glory alone. It is all about Him and His eternal aspirations. Our God reigns for righteousness sake. Our God reigns for the sake of the gospel. Live like He reigns. Live free and by faith. Tell all whom you have earned the right to tell. Your God reigns. Validate your words with your life of faith and faithfulness. Your God reigns. He reigns now and for evermore. Amen and amen!

REFLECTIONS

_____

_____

_____

_____

_____

_____

35

MASTER MEDITATION

Within your temple, O God, we meditate on your unfailing love.
Psalm 48:9

Wise men and women meditate on God. There is a heart and a passion to hear from Him. This is the goal of meditation. It is a process of really listening to the Lord. And the primary purpose for listening is for the transformation of the hearer. It is not to gain more information so we can impress others with our knowledge, which pride promotes. Our flesh wants to leverage listening for our own advantage. We sometimes only listen so we can size up someone or something. We try to determine how we can persuade others to our way of thinking. So listening becomes a lever for personal advantage rather than personal transformation. The Lord loathes this low level of listening. His desire is for us to listen to Him and others for the purpose of becoming more like Jesus. Our Master's desire is for us to master meditation for the purpose of His mastery over our life.

If we are not careful we cringe at the thought of what Christ may say and we only listen to what we want to hear. However, selective listening is not satisfactory to our Savior. Meditation means we listen to the full counsel of God. It is indiscriminate in its understanding of God's character and His personal purpose for you. So when you get quiet before Christ you cannot pick and choose what you want to appropriate to your life. In fact, our Heavenly Father's passion is much more than His children just applying truth to their lives. It is engagement. Meditation on our Master leads to massive transformation. It unleashes a work of grace in our heart that gyrates to the next generations. Meditation on God becomes the Spirit's system for governing your life.

Furthermore, we meditate personally and corporately. We individually hear God speak. His intimacy is unrivaled in the way He loves us specifically for who we are. Personally He has a plan and a purpose that we come to appreciate and understand in solitude and silence. But we also meditate on our Master among the masses. This is our gathering for collective praise and worship. Our spirit engages with His transcendence and holiness through the coming together with other believers in bold proclamation of our belief.

Moreover, dig out time daily for meditation on your Master. Listen to Him thorough His written word. This is a personal letter from your Heavenly Father that oozes in His unfailing love. Secondly, listen to Him through the life of the living word, Jesus (John 1:14). He is God incarnate. When we encounter Christ we are wise to be transformed by His grace.

Lastly, listen to the Lord through writing. Journal what Jesus is saying to you. Pen to paper pulls out what is within your heart. It exposes you to who you are and who He is, and how you can become more like Him. Consider calendaring a weekend of worship with Christ. The more you meditate on His unfailing love, the more you are loved by Him. And, the more you are capable to fulfill His greatest command of loving Him and loving others. Meditation migrates us toward our Master Jesus. It is His tool of transformation. Authentic meditation moves us to be mastered by our Master!

REFLECTIONS

_____

_____

_____

_____

_____

_____

36

HONOR GOD

*He who sacrifices thank offerings honors me, and he prepares the way
so that I may show him the salvation of God.*
Psalm 50:23

Honor of God is our obligation as Jesus followers. It is not an option but an opportunity to afford praise and thanksgiving to the Almighty. The honor of God places the focus of our appreciation on the object of our affection, Jesus. It is way beyond just the mere morsels of language from our lips (Mark 7:6). The honor of God is meant to be a habit of our living. Our life reeks in honor when our attitude of gratitude sets the tone for our actions. It is honorable to God when we are grateful for our jobs and the people with whom we work. We take the time to celebrate birthdays and verbally affirm the character traits of the one being honored. This small scenario of gratitude honors our Savior. It is a celebration of salvation in the life of one of His children. Gratitude honors God.

Our worship honors God when our behavior matches our beliefs. This is why we come before Christ in confession and repentance. It is an honoring of the standards He has set with His life and word. It is dishonoring to our Lord to receive Jesus at salvation and then ignore Him until we get to heaven. Our enemies get more attention than this lowly form of ingratitude. We go to God because we need it and He deserves and expects it. The simple act of submission and surrender to Jesus honors Him in heaven and on earth. If the angels bow before Him, how much more should we (Psalm 103:20)? Holy living submits its whole way to divine direction. We honor heaven when we ask God for guidance.

Indeed it is out of our honoring of God and others that He shows us the way. Honor is a highway to heaven (Philippians 3:20). It is in our acts of honor that we hear the voice of the one we are honoring. Honoring improves our hearing. Honoring brings clarity. It is when we honor God and people above ourselves that we gain perspective (Romans 12:9-10). Self-honoring sucks out life from a situation while offering honors gives life. It honors others when we serve them. It honors others when we are kind. It honors others when we involve them in the decision making process. It honors others when we invite them to special occasions like showers, weddings, funerals and anniversaries. It honors others when we celebrate what is important to them. Honor helps others understand.

Furthermore honor God with your body (I Corinthians 6:20). Our body is a reflection of God. It is His and He expects it to be in its best condition. When we care for our body we care for Christ. It honors Him. It is also unacceptable to the Almighty when we abuse our body. When we abuse our body we abuse Christ. Therefore, honor Him in your body. Dress so you draw attention to your inner beauty. This honors Him.

Lastly, God honors those who honor Him (1 Samuel 2:30). What an honor to be honored by God. He honors us with His intimacy. He honors us with responsibilities and success. He honors us with wisdom. He honors us with blessings undeserved. He honors us with friends and family. He honors us with health and healing. He honors us by calling us His own. Our honor invites His honor. By God's grace do the honorable thing. Honor prepares His way!

REFLECTIONS

_____

_____

_____

_____

_____

_____

37

BROKEN BY GOD

The sacrifices of God are a broken spirit; a broken and a contrite heart,
O God, you will not despise.
Psalm 51:17

Brokenness by God is beautiful to Him. It is His passageway to purity. It is His entrance into intimacy. It is His plan for our maturity in the faith. However, it is painful and not pretty at times. We can become stubborn and selfish in our way of doing things. We need the tender touch of our Lord to lead us away from a hardening heart to one that is broken before Him. An unbroken heart rivals God. A broken heart aligns with God. Unbroken, we are like a stallion in the wild. We need a 'heart whisperer' from heaven to tame our spirit. We need God's bridle of brokenness to bring us under submission. If we buck the breaking of the Holy Spirit, then we are in for a rougher ride. Why push back with pride when the outcome can be joy and gladness with God? He breaks us to build us up.

Indeed some things that are broken are discarded. They are done away with because they are more easily replaced than repaired. We can't drink any longer from a broken glass. It is useless to its user and discarded. Our heart on the other hand is not useful until it is broken. When broken by God the heart can no longer be adamant to do its own thing. A heart is never at its best until it is broken. Brokenness brings out what is on the inside. It reveals where there is still a rascal in rebellion. It is in our brokenness that divine restoration takes place. A heart becomes whole when it is broken. This is the Lord's way. He doesn't break us and leave us to suffer in pain and discomfort. It is out of our brokenness that He pulls us close to His heart in compassion and love.

Moreover, brokenness is both an event and a process. Your salvation broke you of unbelief and brought you into right standing with your Savior. However, the Holy Spirit is still breaking your behavior by conforming you into the image of Christ. It is a process of your pride decreasing and your humility increasing. Do not be gullible in thinking you are over the need for a work of God's grace. Brokenness is a process of becoming more like Jesus. Your Christian maturity didn't occur when you were first broken; it began. Brokenness brings us back to our faith in Him. He tames us to trust Him. Therefore, out of your brokenness present to your Savior the sacrifice of a contrite heart. It may be financial brokenness, relational brokenness, emotional brokenness, or physical brokenness. Wherever the pain is present it to Him for healing. He restores broken hearts.

Lastly, do not be afraid of brokenness. Invite it as a blessing instead of ignoring it as a burden. It is better to be broken a little along the way that a lot out in one fail swoop. Brokenness is God's way to blessing and change. He breaks our will and restores us into the wisdom of His will. He breaks our spirit and restores us into the security of His Spirit. He breaks our pride and restores us into His humility. He breaks our stubbornness and restores us into His sensitivity. He breaks our harshness and restores us into His kindness. He breaks our greed and restores us into His generosity. He breaks our lust and restores us into His love. He breaks our disobedience and restores us into His obedience. Brokenness is our transformation by His grace and truth. God breaks us to conform us into the image of His son!

REFLECTIONS

_____

_____

_____

_____

_____

_____

38

TRUST GROWS

But I am like an olive tree flourishing in the house of God;
I trust in God's unfailing love for ever and ever.
Psalm 52:8

Trust is the soil in which our faith grows. Like a robust olive tree full of branches bearing luscious fruit, trust causes growth across the limbs of our life. It is trust that tears down our walls of fear. It is trust that allows us to outlast our critics. It is trust that brings to fruition a harvest of hope and patience. It is trust that keeps us from reacting wrongly. It is trust that moves a man to forgive his wife, or a wife to forgive her husband. It is trust that stands the test of time. Trust causes good things to grow. Our faith grows. Our humility grows. Our love grows. Our holiness grows. Our grace grows. Our fear of God grows. Our character grows. It is trust in our Savior that grows us up for His glory.

God's unfailing love can be trusted, there is no doubt about its trustworthiness. His love never fails (1 Corinthians 13: 8). No one has ever overdrawn the Almighty's account of love. The Lord's loans of love are not called in the middle of your crisis. On the contrary, He gives more love the more needy you find yourself. You can depend on the love of God. It will not fail you when you need Him the most. Others may walk away when you lose your way, but not the love of God; it stays with you. You may feel deserted in your despair but God's love is still there for your comfort and care. His 100% track record of no failures can always be trusted. His love fails not. Our Savior's love is fail-safe.

Sometimes it is hard to see the forest of our Heavenly Father's love, for the trees of terror that stare us in the face. This is where we need to take a time out and trust. Trust God still loves you even when you represent Him poorly. Trust He still loves you even though those around you don't seem to care. Trust He still loves you in the loss of your job. Trust He still loves you though you let Him down. Trust His love does not keep accounts (nor should ours). Furthermore, He loves you so you can be loved and love others on His behalf. Being loved by God is just the beginning. Christians are a conduit for Christ in His cycle of love. We are His love agents, always investigating ways we can extend our Father's love. Love held on to loses it luster. Love given away gains more momentum. So pass along God's unfailing love.

Your trust in Jesus causes your love to grow to greater heights. His goal is for the fruit of His love to weigh down branches of your belief. Your fruitful loving life becomes attractive and inviting to others. They want to draw near the light of the Lord's love that shines through your soul. They want to be close to your character so they can pluck some of your lovely fruit and partake. It is the love of God spread abroad in your life that becomes a beacon of hope. When you unleash love in your life, your faith leadership and ministry will flourish. The fruit of love calms angry hearts. It leads others to forgive and be forgiven. Love allows us to say things we otherwise would not say for fear of hurting another or being rejected. Love is a remedy for rebellion. When the prodigal came home, his father first loved him (Luke 15:20). Love is our first and last response. It is our glimpse into the heart of God. Love never fails because it is guaranteed by God. Indeed, trusting in God's unfailing love grows us up!

REFLECTIONS

_____

_____

_____

_____

_____

_____

39

FOOLISH DENIAL

The fool says in his heart, "There is no God". They are corrupt,
and their ways are vile; there is no one who does good.

Psalm 53:1

Fools foolishly deny God. Deity's denial is the default of the degenerate. It is an excuse for loose living without the Lord. It is the rejection of righteousness. It is their hope that there is no God. Somehow godless belief justifies godless behavior. Denial of God is a push back against His principles. To deny God is to deny His law. Denial of God's law leads to moral and ethical anarchy. There is no stability in a society where everyone does what is right in his or her own eyes (Judges 21:25). Atheism is an excuse to do our own thing. There is no new atheism. It is all old and foolish. It is corrupt in the eyes of Christ.

Corrupt is the how God describes those who deny Him. They are corrupt and vile. These are not just nice people who have lost their way. They shake their faithless fist in the face of God and demand that He disappear. This is what they did to Jesus. He came claiming to be the Christ. He was the Messiah for the salvation of mankind. But some men did not want God. They were a 'god' unto themselves. So they paid back Jesus evil for good. They also made fun of the men and women who by faith followed Him. Some were so offended by His teachings that they ran Him out of town. He taught submission to God's authority over their list of man-made rules. He made the undercover atheists irate because He rivaled their authority and power. So they attempted to kill God. But Christ's crucifixion drove the final nail into the coffin of their nihilism, after three days He came alive. God is not dead. It's peculiar that corruption tries to kill others but wounds itself.

As a follower of Jesus you may feel the pressure from outside forces to deny Him. There is no need to go there. Do not allow the persuasion of unprincipled people to force you into a faithless box. Atheism is for the uninformed. How can someone deny the existence of God when his or her understanding of all knowledge is relatively minimal? An atheist can only 'say' in their heart, while Christians can 'know' in their heart. We know because the evidence for God is overwhelming. We know because we have experienced God. We know because we know Him. Like Paul we are persuaded to remain faithful because of God's faithfulness (2 Timothy 1:12 KJV). Belief in the absence of God is foolish. It is the opium of the uninformed. Belief in God is wisdom. It is what makes sense out of life.

Lastly, be there for those when they finally figure out that atheism is not working for them. It may be a crisis that turns them to Christ. It may be a respected relationship that they begin to see authentic faith lived out and they desire the same. It may be reading the Holy Scriptures and mining out mounds of Gospel gold that point them to their Heavenly Father. Pray for the Holy Spirit to penetrate the deceived heart of an atheist. God wants all men to be saved and come to the knowledge of the truth (1 Timothy 2:4). Furthermore, the reality of God shines through you and melts away their denial. Your faith is a reality check for fools. Wisdom is the way to God. Spirit-filled Christians are a compelling case for Christianity. You are an attractive advocate for Almighty God. Therefore, love atheists to the Lord!

REFLECTIONS

_____

_____

_____

_____

_____

_____

40

PERSEVERANCE PATTERN

Surely God is my help, the Lord is the one who sustains me.
Psalm 54:4

Our Savior sustains us by His strength. Christ causes us to carry on with His compassionate care. Our Heavenly Father is forever loving us to Himself; and then sending us forth into the fray by faith. And the Holy Spirit is our Helper (Romans 8:26). The Lord leverages our life for His longevity. His desire is for us to not give in or give up. He is a God of determination and He expects His children to do the same. Indeed, the Almighty's aid is better than all the help of men. Heaven's help stands ready to sustain you. It is in prayer that you perceive God's help and persevere. Perseverance is a product of seeing your circumstances from Christ's perspective. It produces peace and a quiet confidence (Isaiah 32:17). Indeed we have a divine champion in whom we can be confident.

We have no need to fret because our Heavenly Father is here to help. Sometimes the pressures at work pour over you like the constant pelting of golf ball size hail. You are bruised; beat up and unsure of yourself. The nick picking of people makes you feel like you are about to be nibbled to death by ducks. Nothing seems to be going right so you begin to conclude that you need to quit. However, don't quit before God is done with you. His 'will' may be for you to persevere in your pain. The Bible teaches, "You need to persevere so that when you have done the will of God, you will receive what he has promised" (Hebrews 10:36). Hang in there so you don't miss out on what heaven has for you. God's best may be yet to come. Furthermore, we persevere in our pain in order to grow our character. Paul understood this principle of perseverance. He said, "...we also rejoice in our sufferings, because we know that suffering produces perseverance; perseverance, character; and character, hope" (Romans 5:3-4).

God is our help in times of trouble. He is whom we trust. We persevere when we see Him. It is easy for our eyesight to become preoccupied with problems. Our immediate issues can overwhelm us, if we allow them that unhealthy level of influence. But the Lord would rather have us linger with Him. Replace unproductive time of worry with productive time in prayer. When you gaze on God fears fade away. The writer of Hebrews captured this confidence in the life of Moses, "By faith he left Egypt, not fearing the king's anger; he persevered because he saw him who is invisible" (Hebrews 11:27). Little do we care for the defiance of our foes when we have the defense of God.

God's grace will sustain you. His grace is sufficient for your specific situation. You can move forward by faith. Do not allow this financial set back to keep you from going to God. He owns everything. He has what you need to make it through this transition. God is already on your side, so stay by His. You have His mammoth mercy and loving kindness to draw on in your discouragement. The help of people comes and goes, but the Lord perseveres with you, so you can persevere with Him. Your Savior, not stuff, is your sustainer. Be encouraged by heaven's help. Remain steadfast with God. He is... with you!

REFLECTIONS

_____

_____

_____

_____

_____

_____

41

A FRIEND'S REJECTION

If an enemy were insulting me, I could endure it; if a foe were raising himself
against me, I could hide from him. But it is you, a man like myself,
my companion, my close friend with whom I once enjoyed sweet fellowship
as we walked with the throng at the house of God.
Psalm 55:12-14

The worst kind of rejection may be the rejection of a friend. You expect it from an enemy, but not from a friend. It doesn't make sense that someone you communed with around Christ, would come back and crush you with rejection. Rejection integrated with religious pretense is rough. It challenges our trust in people in general, and our faith in God in particular. With an open foe you can see it coming, however with a pretend friend it takes you by surprise. You feel ambushed by unauthentic living. One day you are laughing together around life's little peculiarities, and the next day you are dazed by the anger of an unstable man. It is haunting and humbling at the same time. You don't know whether to lash back, or to languish in disillusionment. Friendly betrayal is frightening.

Reproaches from those we have been intimate with cut to the quick. They know our strengths and our weaknesses. They know where we are vulnerable. They know how to exploit our struggles, and take advantage of our good will. It is like you have been emotionally naked with someone, and now you feel embarrassed because of his or her indiscretions. What happened to the person you once knew? How could you have been so deceived? It may have been a decade of deceit embedded in your marriage vows. It may have been financial fraud and embezzlement over a long period of time. It may be a hidden addiction that has all the while hijacked your relationship for their creditability.

Our Lord Jesus of course had one for whom he trusted to the point of managing the money. He was close to Christ in proximity, but far away in faith. For Judas it was all about the cash. It was money that motivated him in the beginning, and money that was his downfall in the end. Money motivated men may be pleasant on the outside, but they are full of themselves on the inside. They set you up for their own selfish plan. We see it after the fact. It is so clear. But in the beginning we can be easily deceived. Therefore, really get to know someone before you heavily invest. In time they can be trusted.

Lastly, avoid the temptation to reject those who have rejected you. This is our natural response. However under the influence of the Holy Spirit our right response is to forgive their failings, regardless of how radical their behavior. We are all candidates for sin, even gross sin. Without God's grace and the accountability of a committed community of believers, we are deceivers with the best of them. The worst deceivers have been the most deceived. Paul stated well our role toward those trapped in sin, "Brothers, if someone is caught in a sin, you who are spiritual should restore him gently. But watch yourself, or you also may be tempted" (Galatians 6:1). Yes rejection by a trusted friend is fiendish and false hearted. However we are called to be forgiving and pure hearted. Do not stoop to their standards that are sub par with your Savior's. By God's grace rise above rejection!

REFLECTIONS

42

PURPOSE FULFILLMENT

I cry out to God Most High, to God, who fulfills his purpose to me.
Psalm 57:2

Providence has a personal purpose for His people. Our gracious God guarantees a grant of wisdom into His ways. He wants us to experience His eternal aims for His glory. Paul stated this principle of providential purpose fulfillment crystal clear when he stated with conviction, "...being confident of this, that he who began a good work in you will carry it on to completion until the day of Christ Jesus" (Philippians 1:6). His purpose fulfillment started when we placed our faith in Jesus. This was our contract with Christ that placed the responsibility of fulfilling His purpose at the feet of our Heavenly Father. Our Lord finishes anything and everything He has begun since our belief in Him. Whatsoever the Lord takes in hand, He will accomplish. So we trust the Almighty with the fulfillment of His purpose for our life. Therefore, it is imperative that we intercede to understand Him.

Prayer positions us to harvest heaven's purpose for our life. We cry out to the Most High because there is nothing, or no one, any higher. He is at the top. He is the divine decision maker. He is our Maker. There is no one else we can go to for an understanding of the purpose of providence for our life than the Lord Jesus Christ. Faith is not dumb. We pray because we believe there is a better way than our very limited wisdom. We can get by with the wisdom of the world, but we can thrive with the wisdom of Almighty God. We cry out to Christ because He has adopted us. He is our Heavenly Father from whom we define our purpose by His purpose for us. Prayer pulls out His purpose front and center.

Prayer to God is proof of our trust in God. When we send our prayers to heaven, God will send help down from heaven. Unless we pray, as well as trust, our trust will fail us. Trust can become trivial if persistent prayer does not back it up. Prayer brings trust into the reality of God's promises and purpose for our life. Prayer is potent because it aligns us with the purposes of Almighty God. Moreover, once we understand His personal purpose, we can rest assured of His follow through of its fulfillment on our behalf. Furthermore, put pen to paper and prayerfully define your God-given purpose. Use this definition as a filter for decision-making. This becomes your accountability to God and others to say 'no'.

Lastly, lean into the Lord to lead you in His purpose for your life. Once you establish His purpose for you, leverage that for others. Use your strength of position to help others discover their God-given purpose. Have them list their gifts, skills, passions and experiences. Pray with them of how God wants to collate their assets for Christ. Assure them that their Heavenly Father will fulfill His purpose for them, as He did with His own son at just the right time (Galatians 4:4, NASB). Be patient in the implementation of God's purpose for your life. Remember you are living His purpose now. No season of life is insignificant in the Lord's eyes. Don't wish away where you are today. By faith, you can be sure that Christ is currently fulfilling your purpose. Make sure your goals are God-given and then trust Him with their fulfillment. A prayerful purpose is patient with God!

REFLECTIONS

_____

_____

_____

_____

_____

_____

43

POISONOUS PRIDE

Their venom is like the venom of a snake, like that of a cobra that
has stopped its ears, that will not heed the tune of the charmer,
however skillful the enchanter may be.
Psalm 58:4-5

Pride is poisonous in its effect. Like a slithering snake, it sneaks up on its prey and delivers its deadly venom with a startling and painful bite. Its venom travels quickly to all parts of the body with paralyzing impact. Without the salvation of a properly applied serum, the victim's life is sadly snuffed out. This is why it is wise to be ever vigilant by staying on the look out for pride. Pride may be quietly coiled in the bushes of our heart when a crisis causes it to lash out. Pride slithers through our selfish desires and strikes back when we do not get our way. Pride doesn't listen because it has its mind made up; others become the enemy if they disagree. Pride is deadly. It kills relationships and strikes fear in those in its path. Pride is a natural response to someone whose security lies outside their Savior.

Pride's insecurity lies in a false faith. You cannot be authentically intimate with Jesus and remain secure in your self. True communion with Christ transfers our trust to Him. He then transforms us into humble and obedient followers. This is one reason Paul says, "Do not conform any longer to the pattern of this world, but be transformed by the renewing of your mind" (Romans 12:2a). It takes time, but the serum of humility eventually overtakes the poison of pride, and makes us rest secure in Christ. Left unchecked, our proud insecurities lead to a hard heart, a stiff neck and stopped up ears.

Pride does not listen to the logic of counsel that is contrary to its conclusions. Sadly, a closed mind leads to a joyless heart. It is not a matter of who is right or wrong. The humble ask, "What is the wise thing to do?" "What is best for the enterprise, the team or the family?" Otherwise, we get wrapped around the axle of anger, if pride is not recognized and repented of immediately. It is hard to see pride in the mirror, but it is easy to see it in someone else. Therefore, loosen your grip on controlling outcomes, and really listen to all involved. Love and respect means we listen well. How can we be truly hearing from our Heavenly Father, if we cannot hear from His children? Listening to the Lord requires listening to those around us. He speaks through the stakeholders in our lives. Our spouse, our parents, our children, our peers, our friends and even acquaintances can all be God's messengers of mercy. The enemy is our poisonous pride, not people.

Lastly, come clean with Christ with a contrite and teachable heart. Die to being right, and come alive to honoring others by inviting their contrary thinking. There is no need to fear questions. It is the dismissed or overlooked wise and discerning questions that we should worry about. Even if the questioner carries pride, resist the temptation to defend. Allow the process to prove what's right. A thoughtful and respectful process reaps the right results. Indeed, humility listens intently, understands thoroughly and responds appropriately. In prayer, we listen to the Lord. In conversation, we listen to people. Humility values both of these channels of wisdom. By God's grace, avoid the pain of pride before it strikes!

REFLECTIONS

_____

_____

_____

_____

_____

_____

44

REQUEST FOR RESTORATION

You have rejected us, O God, and burst forth among us;
you have been angry—now restore us!
Psalm 60:1

Restoration means we are in right relationship with God and others. When we come to the end of ourselves we are in a position to request restoration with God. Restoration with God is the right request, but it happens when we are willing to come clean with Christ. We cannot simultaneously be restored by God and rebel against God. It doesn't work this way in the Lord's economy of relational wholeness. Restoration follows repentance. When the one running from God finally grows weary, they are then ready for repentance. Furthermore, our inaction to obey is offensive to omnipotent God. It is our obedience that honors Him. It is our obedience that positions us for restoration. Disobedience invites rejection, while obedience invites restoration. Indeed, restoration requires obedience.

Disobedience forms a breach in our beliefs. It causes cracks in an already fragile faith in Christ. Disobedience dismisses doctrine as too restraining. Disobedience declares itself superior to its Savior. It thinks it has a better plan than Providence. Sometimes we are our own worse enemy. Indeed, disobedience is disillusioned and foolish. It forgets to apply simple faith in Christ. It overlooks the wisdom of obedience and replaces it with the foolishness of disobedience. When we fail to obey, we open ourselves up to a failure of faith. A fractured faith needs restoration by God. Only heaven can heal a broken heart.

Moreover, a state of disobedience is fatiguing, while obedience energizes. Our soul becomes sluggish under the weight of going our own way. Disobedience is like swimming up stream in a raging river. It is like fighting against the wicked under-tow of an ocean's crosscurrents. The design of life is not to be lived in defiance to the will of the Lord. We are wired to walk with Him, not ignore Him, or run away from Him. Rejection from another may have repelled you to run from them and God. But now it is time to come back to Christ. His restoration is the remedy for your seething soul. Boiling bitterness burns everyone and everything in its path. Turn down the heat of hate and become restored.

Lastly, obedience leads to the opportunity for restoration. Forgive the sin and smile once again. You have probably been wronged, and you may not totally understand the extent of your hurt, so ask God to reveal how you hurt and where you need forgiveness. Start by asking God to forgive you, so you in turn can forgive others. It is lonely without the Lord's presence, wisdom and blessing. Come back to Him for relational restoration. Remember the joy of your salvation and celebrate it with Christ. Weep with gratitude for what God has given you. Things will not be the same as they once were, but by God's grace they can be better. The scars of sin may never go away, but the beauty of restoration can over shadow them. Restoration is not a one-time occurrence, but the process of a lifetime of obedience. You cannot control the outcomes of others, but you can allow Christ to control you. Relish His restoration. Live to linger under the Lord's influence. Those restored are not bored. Once restored by God, you can help others reap the rewards of their own restoration!

REFLECTIONS

_____

_____

_____

_____

_____

_____

45

RICH AFFECTION

Though your riches increase, do not set your heart on them.
Psalm 62:10b

Money is a lover who romances us regularly. It seeks seduction over our emotions. It promises security though its outcome is uncertain (Proverbs 23:5). It promises satisfaction, but it is never content (Ecclesiastes 5:10). It promises hope, but real hope is found in seeking first God's Kingdom (Matthew 6:33). It promises worldly wealth, but true riches remain in a growing relationship with Jesus (Luke 16:11). It promises you a non-compete with Christ, however it is the number one competitor to our communion with Christ (Matthew 6:24). Money is a lover that leads us astray. It plays with our heart, and then without notice breaks our heart. Money has no conscience. It is a selfish lover.

Therefore, beware of the raw deal riches offer. Do not become seduced by the sirens of power and pride. We are the same people we were before our net worth went on the rise. We were saved by grace to get us to heaven, and we depend on grace daily to get us along on earth. Yes, we have more unique issues and opportunities, because we have extra money. But God's extras are first meant for the eternal. It is not about feeding our 'me monster' with more and more. Affection of riches leads us to overindulge ourselves. Its like our loyalty shifts from loving the Lord, to loving stuff. Because we have extra we limit the Lord, and excess ourselves with unnecessary accessories. Do we really need the next version, or the latest brand? Will we die without the latest and the greatest? Be clear. Ambiguous affections are unacceptable to our Lord. Most of us have been blessed with more than we need. Make sure your riches lead you into a deeper love relationship with the Gift Giver, and not in love with the gifts in which you have been richly blessed.

Moreover, riches without a game plan are irresponsible to God. Riches rule, unless there is a wise and prayerful plan. A plan relegates them to a place of submission to God's ways. Begin engaging in a Bible study about money, and learn your role as a steward of God's stuff. Consider hiring a financial planner who can hold you accountable to stay fiscally pure to a Kingdom paradigm of planning. Predetermine to be a predictable percentage giver. The Bible teaches the principle of steady plodding (Proverbs 21:5 LB). Emotional giving alone is immature giving. Graduate to a mature giver who is proactive, and not just reactive. Wise giving has a guaranteed eternal return on investment.

Lastly, lead others to love the Lord and not wealth. Be a role model to your children and peers. Trust God and not your wealth. Riches have never been true to those who trusted in them. They are themselves transient things; therefore they deserve our transient thoughts. Cleave to Christ, not alluring riches that entangle and complicate your life. Jesus is the lover of your soul, not stuff. So, place all your affection on Him and not on those things that will let you down (Colossians 3:1-3 KJV). Don't fall in love with that which perishes. Fall in love with the One who keeps you from perishing. Perish the thought we would trust money over our Master. Almighty God is our rich affection!

REFLECTIONS

_____

_____

_____

_____

_____

_____

46

EARNEST SEEKER

O God, you are my God, earnestly I seek you, my soul thirsts for you,
my body longs for you, in a dry and weary land, where there is no water.
Psalm 63:1

God is ours because we are His. He is our personal God. He wants us to approach Him and address Him as "My God". This is what children do with their parents; they address them as my mom and my dad. It honors most parents to be personally addressed by a loving and grateful child. This is how Christians are to approach their Heavenly Father. Christians can earnestly approach heaven and state their need to 'my God'. Firm faith allows us to claim Him as our own. We possess God because He possesses us. Possession breeds desire. Full assurance of access to our Heavenly Father does not hinder diligence, but encourages earnestness. We seek after our own. We seek earnestly and we seek early.

Indeed, earnest seekers of their Savior can't wait to be with Jesus. Early in the morning they want to encounter the love of God. Before the grassy dew is sucked up from the sun's heat, they want to be lifted up by the warm love of the Lord. He removes any wet residue of worry from our soul. Like the chill of the morning, He takes away any fears that may have cooled our faith. Morning time with our Master is manna from Heaven. God provided manna for His children Israel. It quenched their souls thirst and fed their hungry bodies. But the manna dissolved if it was not gathered early in the day (Exodus 16:21). In the same way, we are to earnestly seek our Savior's eternal agenda at the beginning of each day, or His directions dissolve into the busyness of our schedules. Harvest your Master's manna before the manna of man has time to substitute its weak wisdom. His morning manna is fresh and full of faith. Earnestly seek Him. He satisfies your soul.

You may discover your soul is in a weary spot of worry. But weariness makes the presence of God more desirable. We become desperate for God when the fatigue of life parches our thirsty souls. When outward comforts are absent, we can continue as we walk in the inward serenity of our Savior Jesus. You may feel totally alone right now, because no one seems to understand or accept your point of view. You feel undervalued and underappreciated. It some ways you have become a mercenary for the mission of the organization. You only show up for the paycheck and your patience has run thin. It is not worth having to fight all the time for what's right. But Christ is calling you to Himself during this time of vocational disconnect. Learn how to love, when you are not being loved. Learn how to understand, when you are not being understood. Learn how to serve, when you are not being served. We earnestly seek God, so we have energy for others.

Lastly, earnest seekers know what to do when they find their Heavenly Father. They rest. They reflect. They enjoy. They allow Him to rejuvenate their sickly soul. Do the same. As you seek Him, you will find Him (Deuteronomy 4:29). When you find Him, allow Him to be your Father. Trust Him to love you, as only He can. Trust Him to correct you, as only He can. Trust Him to forgive you, as only He can. Trust Him to lead you, as only He can. Earnestly seek God, because He earnestly cares. Seekers enjoy satisfaction!

REFLECTIONS

_____

_____

_____

_____

_____

_____

47

PONDER AND PROCLAIM

*All mankind will fear; they will proclaim the works of God and
ponder what he has done.*
Psalm 64:6

God's works are worth pondering and proclaiming. First we ponder on His works. Once we ponder them, we are compelled to proclaim them. His works are wonderful because they bring glory to Him. Our Heavenly Father is the focus. Christ is the center of attention. God's works revolve around His revelation. God's works are in the wonder of His creation. His signature is the soft pure cloud, etched across the backdrop of a brilliant blue sky. His creativity cuts across all creation with the mind-boggling variety of plants and animals. However, His defining work is you. His work in creating you for Himself, and for His glory is both honoring and humbling. It is honoring to know the Lord brought you into this life for His purposes. It is humbling to think you are here on earth as an ambassador of Almighty God. You are an eternal emissary. You are your Father's child.

Therefore, we ponder His work in us. His work in us just got started at salvation. "... being confident of this, that he who began a good work in you will carry it on to completion until the day of Christ Jesus" (Philippians 1:6). Since you were converted to Christ, God has been at work. He has been at work in and through you to conform you into the likeness of His son Jesus (Romans 8:29). Salvation is not an end in itself. It is just the beginning. So we remain a work in progress. We don't arrive until we get to heaven, where the pinnacle of our purification remains. Nevertheless, while we are away from our heavenly home, we allow the Lord to have His way in our life. His greatest work is transforming us into loving and obedient followers of Jesus

His work in you is wonderful and uplifting to describe. You are redeemed and forgiven by the grace of God (Ephesians 1:7). You are a new creation in Christ (2 Corinthians 5:17). You are God's workmanship, created to produce good works (Ephesians 2:10). You are accepted by Christ (Romans 15:7). In Christ Jesus you have wisdom, righteousness, sanctification and redemption (I Corinthians 1:30).

You are joined to the Lord and are one spirit with Him (I Corinthians 6:17). You are made complete in Christ (Colossians 2:10). Christ is your life (Colossians 3:4). You are set free in Christ (Galatians 5:1). God will supply all your needs (Philippians 4:19). Indeed, God's work is without end.

Lastly, after we ponder the work of God around us, in us and through us, we are compelled to proclaim His faithfulness. Grateful mouths cannot keep shut. We thank Him with a quiet bowed head over meals. We announce His goodness, by exercising good deeds to others. We spread His fame with our unwavering faithfulness to His name. We lift up the Lord when we love others on His behalf. We exclaim obedience and loyalty to Him when we die daily to our own selfish desires and submit to His. Children of God boast about the grandeur and goodness of their Heavenly Father. We can't keep quite because of the worship that erupts from our inner most being. The fear and love of God moves us to ponder on the truth of God, and proclaim the grace of God. Therefore, proclaim God with your life and use words when necessary!

REFLECTIONS

_____

_____

_____

_____

_____

_____

48

ENVIRONMENTAL CONTROLS

You care for the land and water it; you enrich it abundantly.
The streams of God are filled with water to provide the people with grain,
for so you have ordained it.   Psalm 65:9

God created the earth. He cares for the earth. He softens the iron clouds of drought and frees them to fill rivers with rain. Millions of dollars come from heaven in the form of damp dirt on the earth. He cares for the environment. As a result, its inhabitants receive His care. The earth is His. Its fullness is for His glory. Yet, we sometimes soil the environment with our senseless and shortsighted behaviors. However, responsible followers of Jesus respect God's resources. There is energy around engaging with the environment in a healthy fashion. There is foresight in fostering its value beyond today into tomorrow. Environmental controls are right, because they reflect wise stewardship of God's stuff. We have dominion over God's environment (Genesis 1:27-29).

Moreover, we are a product of our environments. There is the corporate environment of Christ's creation, and there are the customized environments we live within every day. Both our general and specific environments influence what we become. If we live in a part of the world that prevents the public worship of Christ then our faith is enclosed, but not any less fervent. The bond of Christian Community is critical in an overall atheistic environment. If our environment is agricultural then there is a direct dependency on God to provide rain at just the right time. Agrarian environments facilitate faith in Almighty God. If your environment is intellectual, then you may thrive on logic and reason.

Therefore, environmental controls make a difference. Who you hang out with determines who you become. "Do not be misled: Bad company corrupts good character" (I Corinthians 15:33). You value what those closest to you value. If they model loose use of money then you may soon discover yourself deep in debt. Indeed, be respectful but cautious when exposed to unhealthy environments. For example, do not take marriage counsel from someone who survived multiple marriages, but didn't seem to learn from their mistakes. Avoid parenting advice from those whose children have a long-term pattern of disrespect, disobedience and who are distant from authority. Instead, value environments of wisdom, love, fear of God, stability and security.

Above all else, God blesses environments that encourage engagement with Him. He is our ultimate keeper of environmental controls. Trust Him to lead you to the places that value what He values. Look for a spouse who loves Jesus more than they love you. Pray for them as you attend Bible studies, serve in the Church or travel on mission trips. Furthermore, you can take the lead by creating environments of encouragement. Ask God to give you the discernment to know how to love those in your sphere of influence. Control your environment by creating your environment. The Holy Spirit working through you creates compelling places that invite others to Christ. The ultimate environment is one that is Christ centric. Therefore, look to the Lord. Trust Him. Expose yourself to healthy environments. And, by God's grace, create environments that honor Christ. Care about environmental controls. Create environments that create character!

REFLECTIONS

_____

_____

_____

_____

_____

_____

49

SIN SILENCES PRAYER

I cried out to him with my mouth; his praise was on my tongue.
If I had cherished sin in my heart, the Lord would not have listened;
but God has surely listened and heard my voice in prayer.
Psalm 66:17-19

Sin is a silencer that shoots down prayer. Our un-confessed sin cancels our communion with Christ. It shatters our souls longing to align with the Almighty. Sin over-promises and under-delivers. It promises you pleasure, but its ultimate outcomes are hollow. It promises you freedom, but it leaves you in bondage. It promises you privileges, but then takes away privileges. Iniquity invites you into its influence, and then hangs you out to dry as you attempt to cry out to God. Indeed, sin is suicidal to your prayer life. Sin and your Savior cannot coexist. It is anti-Christ. Before we pray, we are to come clean with sin. Jesus said it like this, "Therefore, if you are offering your gift at the altar and there remember that your brother has something against you, leave your gift there in front of the altar. First go and be reconciled to your brother; then come and offer your gift" (Matthew 5:23-24). Getting right our relationships precedes getting right with God.

We cannot harbor sin in our heart and expect God to hear our prayers in heaven. Sin confuses and complicates matters. Where there is confusion look out for un-confessed sin. We cannot hear God, because sin has deafened our heart. The eardrums of our soul burst under the pressure of un-confessed sin. Furthermore, sin blocks the door of obedience. As with Cain, sin crouches at the door and hinders our passage. (Genesis 4:7). Therefore, check your motives for coming to Christ in prayer. Make sure it is to manifest His glory and not yours. The half brother of Jesus said, "When you ask, you do not receive, because you ask with wrong motives, that you may spend what you get on your pleasures" (James 4:3). Maturity rids its innermost being of any alliance with iniquity.

Moreover, marriage is fertile ground for un-confessed sin to foster. Be on the look out for sins that wedge themselves in between your intimacy with your spouse. It happens quickly in the rush to discipline children, or in the throngs of making a living. We can easily become disconnected. This is why communication is critical in understanding what sins to confess and why. Husbands who take this lightly risk their prayers being un-answered. Once impetuous Peter said it well, "Husbands, in the same way be considerate as you live with your wives, and treat them with respect as the weaker partner and as heirs with you of the gracious gift of life, so that nothing will hinder your prayers" (I Peter 3:7). This high level of tender care takes time. However, this investment positions a couple's prayer life to experience radical results. Humility leads to unhindered prayers.

Lastly, be assured the Lord listens to and responds to prayers from a pure heart. He invites intimacy. This is who He is, and what He does. He revels in restoring you into right relationship with Himself. His spirit thrives in an unsoiled heart. Therefore, prepare yourself with confession of sin, before you ask anything of your Savior. Ask first for forgiveness from God and man; then go to God in prayerful petition. A pure heart is a prerequisite for supplications to your Savior. Purity positions you for prayer. Repentance of sin allows you to offer up effective prayers. This is first as you faithfully follow Jesus!

REFLECTIONS

_____

_____

_____

_____

_____

_____

50

GOD'S BLESSING RELEASED

*May God be gracious to us and bless us and make his face to shine upon us,
that your ways may be known on earth, your salvation among all nations.*
Psalm 67:1-2

The mercy and grace of God govern our blessings from God. We should not ask for the blessing of God, until we receive forgiveness from God. We do not request the peace of God, until we have made peace with God. We are not invited onto the journey of God's blessing, until we have first been born again. Being born again gives us direct access to the beautiful blessings of our Heavenly Father. God loves to bless the obedient. An earthly high priest spoke his blessing over God's people (Numbers 6:24-25), but it is the blessing of our heavenly High Priest that we cry out to expectantly. Moreover, our Heavenly Father releases His blessing, so we can be a blessing to all nations. We are a blessing pass-through for God. Christ transforms us into an instrument of His blessing.

Indeed, God blesses us to be a blessing to others. Locally, regionally, nationally and globally God wants to unleash His bountiful blessing through His children. If we hang on to His blessing just for ourselves, we risk losing His blessing. The way we retain the blessing of the Lord is by giving it away. We give it away to those who are near, and we give it away to those who are far away. He expects His people to propagate His principles and precepts to all nations. This is what Jesus meant when He said to go into all the world and make disciples by teaching them His ways (Matthew 28:19-20). This strategy assures the Almighty's presence and blessing. His blessing is not confined to one country or language. Christ's blessing belongs in every tribe and tongue who trust Him.

Furthermore, trafficking in God's blessing requires uncommon faith. Uncommon faith sees the face of God. His face shines on His faithful servants. It is a light that leads you to walk in the ways of your Lord. Common faith can see the deeds of God all around, but it is uncommon faith that experiences God. Uncommon faith sees the face of your Heavenly Father, interprets His ways, discerns His plans and lives out His purposes. It is at this point that you are engaged with eternity. Your life's transformation by God reveals His son Jesus to those for whom you are seeking to bless. God's grace is the ultimate gift. This is the best blessing we can bestow on others. It is when people see beyond our good deeds and gifts to the originator of the blessings that we have been successful. We bless others, so they will enter into a relationship with the Blesser.

Lastly, do not linger too long in your country of origin. Venture out into God's vast harvest that is ready for prayed up laborers (John 4:35). Do not sit still waiting for the world to come to you. Go out and overcome your fears by faith. Trust God to keep you safe. Trust God to keep you healthy. Trust God to use you for His glory. You will go overseas to be a blessing, but you will return home blessed. What a way to involve friends and family in faith stretching service. Your gratitude grows when you seek to bless those who are spiritually poor and/or materially poor. Do not be shy in serving the world on behalf of your Savior. He has blessed you to be a blessing to all nations. The revelation of Christ through your life may start a revolution of righteousness. Therefore, be blessed to bless!

REFLECTIONS

51

OUT OF CONTROL

Save me, O God, for the waters have come up to my neck. I sink in the miry
depths, where there is no foothold. I have come into the deep waters;
the floods engulf me. I am worn out calling for help; my throat is parched.
My eyes fail, looking for my God.

Psalm 69:1-3

Like Jesus we sometimes cry out to God, especially if we feel things are out of control. The writer of Hebrews describes well Christ's passionate prayers, "During the days of Jesus' life on earth, he offered up prayers and petitions with loud cries and tears to the one who could save him from death, and he was heard because of his reverent submission" (Hebrews 5:7). We cry out to Christ because we cannot get over our need for God. We need to know He is in control. We need to know what we are experiencing is being allowed by the Almighty. He knows what you are going through, therefore He can be trusted to take care of you. God is in control. He is your hope and He is your help.

It is the sinking feeling of our circumstances that cause us the most consternation. The feeling of being totally out of control sends waves of fear over our faith. We feel like we are drowning in despair. We gasp for God. In water we might swim, but in the mud and mire of being out of control, we appear helpless. Like in the sucking of quicksand you sink. The more you struggle the faster and deeper you sink. Instead, give your struggles over to your Savior Jesus. Be still, so He can lift you up. Like Peter, as he was sinking in the storm, you can cry out in your fears, "Lord save me" (Matthew 14:30).

Furthermore, your fervent prayers may have caused you to become hoarse from talking to heaven. Your conversing with Christ has made your faith raw. Indeed, sometimes your eyes of faith fail you. They wander off watching your Lord and fixate on people and problems. Your eyes of faith fail you when you lose focus on your Heavenly Father. In the world you have trouble. In Jesus you have peace (John 16:33). In the world you have discomfort. In Jesus you have comfort (2 Corinthians 1:3-6). In the world you have darkness. In Jesus you have light (John 9:5). In the world you have insecurity. In Jesus you have security (I John 5:13). In the world you have despair. In Jesus you have hope (I Peter 1:3). In the world you are defeated.

In Jesus you have overcome (I John 5:4-5).

Therefore, cling to Christ for He is in control. Submit to your Savior and trust Him. Use your sensitivity to the Spirit's leading to guide you. He will lead you to desirable destinations. His control complements your freedom. You are free to walk by faith and follow Jesus. There is nothing boring about your Lord. He will keep you engaged in eternal endeavors. Your hope may be deferred, but do not allow it's delay to get you down (Proverbs 13:12). Do not grow tired of trusting. He sees your circumstances and cares. He hears your prayers and will answer. He understands your hurt and will heal. He feels your frustrations and will comfort. Listen for His wisdom. It knocks at the door of discernment. Apply what you know, and wait on Him for what you don't know. Christ is in control. Surrender to Him and receive His stability. Sink in sin, or swim with Him!

REFLECTIONS

_____

_____

_____

_____

_____

_____

52

HURRY GOD

Yet I am poor and needy, come quickly to me, O God. You are my help
and my deliverer; O Lord, do not delay.
Psalm 70:5

Adversity invites a sense of urgency. We are urgent in our need for God. We are urgent for reassurance of God's presence and relief from our stressful situation. We are urgent for help from heaven. In our prayers we cry out to Christ. We plead with Him to take away our pain. This is the nature of the needy. We need God. We need God's unselfishness in our marriages. We need God's wisdom in our work. We need God's patience in our dealings with people. We need God's accountability in our integrity. We need to trust God in our troubles. So, out of our pain, our prayers shout for something from our Savior. We need to know He is near—we need to know now.

It is in our poverty of spirit that we see the greatest need for God. It is in our weakness that we are the most teachable to God's wisdom. Our spiritual eyes are clearly focused on our utter dependence on Christ. Ironically, in God's economy, our poverty becomes our wealth (Revelation 2:9) and our weakness becomes our strength (Hebrews 11:34). You may find your faith faltering under the weight of financial conflict. The integrity of your money management is suspect. Your heart hurts, because there is not an alignment around your belief about avoiding debt, and the burden of debt that is weighing down on your wallet. Lack of planning promotes urgency. You are extremely needy for your Heaven Father to fix your finances.

However, what took years to incur may take years for you to dig out of your financial hole. A financial crisis is Christ's opportunity to share with you His 'true riches' (Luke 16:11). He will make haste to walk with you through your money mess. His presence is your best prescription during a time of financial illness. Your Heavenly Father is your provider. His principles of money management are proven. Debt is bad. Giving is good. Saving is wise. Moreover, use this opportunity of humility to reach out to others who are wise in their finances. Let them mentor you in money matters. Their financial 'street smarts' can serve you well. Furthermore, be bold and invite a professional financial planner to provide you accountability and sound advice. Experts with character are a sound resource for wise living. We involve God, when we involve others.

Lastly, maintain a sense of urgency for the Lord at all times. In reality, we are always in desperate need of Him. Dependency on God is not conditional on a crisis. Our requirement for walking with Jesus is our ability to breathe. Maintain a motivation for your Master without having to experience pain first. Pre-pain we can still fervently pray and seek Him. The good times require God as much as the bad times. Your felt need may not be as strong, but reality requests an intimate relationship with your Lord. Use times of stability to go deep with your Savior. Be in a hurry to understand heaven's agenda, especially when things are going well. How wise it is to invite God in when you don't feel the need. Hurry up and gain God's perspective. Be quick to call on Him while things are still calm. Prayerful preparation now will preclude panic in a future crisis. Then you are in a position to prayerfully request by faith, 'Come, Lord Jesus' (Revelation 22:20)!

REFLECTIONS

53

WOMB TO TOMB

For you have been my hope, O Sovereign Lord, my confidence since youth.
From birth I have relied on you; you brought me forth from my mother's womb.
I will ever praise you... Even when I am old and gray, do not forsake me,
O God, till I declare your power to the next generation, your might to all
who are to come.   Psalm 71:5-6, 18

From our mother's womb to our deadly tomb, we have the opportunity to trust God. As an infant we are mostly unaware of our 100% dependence on God, but we grow in understanding over time. It began to make sense as a child when we prayed, "God is good, God is great, let us thank Him for our food". There was a child like trust that had no issue with the vastness of God's power and influence. He was our Heavenly Father who loved us, and who graciously received our love. He was in control of our limited world of home, parents, schoolmates, church, friends and neighbors. It was during these impressionable first 20 years that we began to define our theology of God. Sound teaching stressed the Lord's sovereign grace and our hope in Christ. God is our supreme ruler and ultimate authority. He is to be obeyed and worshiped. Christ in you is the hope of glory (Colossians 1:27). He is the Savior of your sins. Christ is your confidence.

Now that we have graduated from those early days of faith exploration, we are commanded to pass on to our progeny the ways of God. As fathers, we are to bring up our children in the 'nurture and the admonition of the Lord' (Ephesians 6:4). Mom and Dad are to instruct and teach their children (Proverbs 1:8). It is sobering to think we represent the Lord to our little ones. This is why we pray together as parents for our sons and daughters. We struggle to know what they need, but He does. God will give us, as parents, the wisdom and instruction that we need for today, so our children are prepared for tomorrow. Indeed, you help them understand about heaven when you create a home that is loving and accepting. You define boundaries so their moldable minds begin to respect authority and embrace obedience. Educate them well with the help of school and church. Growing up by learning of the Lord has lifetime dividends that never stop paying. Remembering and acknowledging God in youth becomes great satisfaction in old age.

Youth well spent is a comfort in old age. You have joyful reflection. There are limited regrets when you go with God. Yes, growing old possesses it's own set of unique challenges. The beauty of your youth begins to bow to the aging process. Your body becomes a burden to your mind. However, do not allow the failure of your eyesight keep you from seeing God. The need for glasses, surgery or more light is what happens with these temporary tents we live within. Therefore, walk in the light as He is in the light (I John 1:7), and your soul will rivet itself clearly onto the glory and the goodness of God. Our strength decays and we walk slower, but Christ is our strength and His pace is perfect. Our mature mind begins to forget names and places. It becomes hard to recollect where we have been. But in our aging it's important that we age well by exchanging the temporal with the eternal. We substitute stubbornness with sensitivity. We replace peevishness with patience. We exchange fear for faith. Instead of lamenting our infirmities, we praise God for the gift of another day. Old age is the time to leverage your gray hair for God. Invest in leaders who lead well. Teach others to trust Him from the womb to the tomb. By God's grace you have, and it's a compelling story to tell!

REFLECTIONS

_____

_____

_____

_____

_____

_____

54

CHILDREN OF THE NEEDY

He will defend the afflicted among the people and save the children of the
needy, he will crush the oppressor.

Psalm 72:4

The children of the needy are needy. Though many times their needs sit in somber silence until they cry for attention. There is nothing that tugs more at the heart than a needy little one. They did not choose their pitiful and poor plight, any more than the blessed progeny of the privileged. Needy children are the unwilling recipients of a raw deal. They lay in bed at night wondering if God is like their father who abandoned them. How could a good God care if He allows abandonment by an uncaring parent? Indeed, the needy parents are all about trying to survive. In many cases it is a single parent struggling in survival mode. The needy are packhorses for others and paupers for themselves. Some discover, that they are dying a thousand deaths because their children suffer.

Sometimes it is divorce that creates needy children. They are conflicted between mom and dad. What began as a heavenly home of service has become a hellish one of selfishness. Neediness engulfs offspring caught in the crossfire of caustic divorce. Broken marriages break the heart of children. They suffer the most though they are the least of the reasons for a busted marriage. While mom and dad try to get their act together, needy children try to get their needs met. They may find love in the right places like church and Christian homes or they may look elsewhere. Wherever the needy are accepted and loved, they will gravitate. Therefore, those of us who have our needs met in Christ are to reach out to the needy. The needy need uu to lead them in the love of the Lord.

The children of the needy cannot be ignored. Jesus modeled this. The Bible says, "Then little children were brought to Jesus for him to place his hands on them and pray for them. But the disciples rebuked those who brought them. Jesus said, "Let the little children come to me, and do not hinder them, for the kingdom of heaven belongs to such as these" (Matthew 19:13-14). Needy children cannot be neglected. We are either a hindrance, or a helper in getting them to heaven and getting heaven to them. Furthermore, God has blessed us with healthy children, so we can reach out to unhealthy ones. There may be a teenager in your life that is currently disconnected from their parents. They need a safe environment of liberating love. Rebellion subsides under a roof of relationship. Your home is a haven for the needy. Steward it well for others.

Lastly, look for ways to love on children of the needy. Invest in their education. Take them to church, so they can hear the love of Jesus and be loved. Play with them at the park and laugh out loud. Let them be children, so they can become children. It takes time for them to trust, as their trust has been crushed. This is why it is difficult for some needy children to trust Christ. They thirst for a trusting example, so stay trustworthy. You can be a bridge for their beliefs. Love on them by being with them. Give them definition and a context. Love defines rules best in a robust relationship. Moreover, expose your children to needy children. It is good for both. Your children develop gratitude and a heart for service. Needy children gain a friend and a model of faithfulness. Everyone wins. Pray for the needy child in your life and then love on them. Jesus invites the needy!

REFLECTIONS

_____

_____

_____

_____

_____

_____

55

PERPLEXED BUT POISED

Surely God is good to Israel, to those who are pure in heart. But as for me,
my feet had almost slipped; I had nearly lost my foothold.
Psalm 73:1-2

God can be perplexing. This is a normal response to Deity. Because His ways are so much larger in scope, our lack of understanding God can push us to the verge of losing hope. We don't understand why our good God is not giving immediate relief to our pain, or the suffering we see others experiencing. We know God is good. But we want His goodness to express itself in ways we can get our arms around. We like for God's ways to be 'cut and dried', we migrate toward a simple and 'buttoned up' belief system. It is at these points of indecisiveness that we need Him the most. Perplexity needs to lead to our purity. An unclear mind can still experience a poised soul. Do not allow your confused state of mind to lead you into temptation. Satan tried to get Jesus to fall by feeding Him lies during His weakened physical state (Matthew 4). Paul was perplexed, but not in despair (2 Corinthians 4:8, KJV). Indeed, purity of heart paves your way during perplexing times.

Furthermore, life can be perplexing. Why did your friend say one thing and do another? Why do you always seem to be under financial pressure? Why are your parents consumed with themselves? Why are your teenagers disengaged and distant? Why does work seem like a dead end road? These nagging questions pull at our heart and cause us to doubt. We even doubt God at times. John the Baptist doubted in the isolation of prison (Luke 7:20). Allow your doubts to drive you toward God and not away from Him. It is in our perplexity that we are positioned to praise Him. It is in our perplexity that we pray to our good God for His will to be done. We resist the temptation to feel ill toward our Heavenly Father. His integrity is intact. There is nothing about God that is not good.

When men or women doubt the righteousness of God their own integrity is vulnerable to compromise. Our feet of faith begin to slip if we do not anchor our hope in Christ. Keep your inner being aligned with God, so your outer character continues to grow. There is a correlation between God's goodness and the pure in heart. The clean-hearted have all things work out for the good (Romans 8:28). This is why you stand against infidelity and stay faithful to your spouse. This is why you keep your body fit and reject drug and alcohol addiction. This is why you steward your finances well through generous giving, systematic saving and wise spending. Perplexity is your opportunity to obey.

Lastly, perplexity is not sin. Just because you are perplexed with something during this present time does not mean you are sinning. But it is a warning to watch out for temptation. 'Take heed, lest you fall...'(I Corinthians 10:12). Guard your thoughts. You cannot prevent the crow from flying over your head, but you can prevent him from making a nest in your hair. Take every thought captive in obedience to Christ (2 Corinthians 10:5). Saturate your mind with truth, so it flushes out the fears and lies that torment your trust in the Lord. Perplexity is part of your walk with Jesus. Stay poised. Don't allow your vexing to become spiritual vertigo. Keep your balance by believing. Your Savior keeps you from slipping and your heavenly Father keeps you from falling!

REFLECTIONS

_____

_____

_____

_____

_____

_____

56

FEELING REJECTED

*Why have you rejected us forever, O God? Why does your anger smolder
against the sheep of your pasture?*
Psalm 74:1

Anger may make you feel rejected, but it can be a push back to what's wrong. Indeed, God's anger is for our protection. However, as recipients of God's righteous anger, we may feel rejected, even though His anger is directed toward our disobedience and not us. He still loves us as His children when we drift from His best. Sometimes in our fear or frivolity we flee from His influence. Or more subtly and subconsciously, we may daily drift in the wrong direction. Whether sudden or surreal, when we are outside the will of God, we wander into dangerous territory. It is terrible terrain because it is void of the blessing of God. It angers Him when He sees His children stray from the shadow of His saving grace. Why do we go there, when we know it is unsafe and we become fair game for the devil? Adventure away from the Almighty is unwise. Sheep need their shepherd.

Jesus is the Shepherd of your soul. He is the great Shepherd (Hebrews 13:20). Indeed, shepherds 'worth their salt' see to it that their sheep are properly fed, watered and protected from the elements. They care for them, because they care for them. When a sheep strays from the herd, it first startles the shepherd into action. He searches for them with determination. Once they are found there is relief, but anger if they walked away on their on accord. Anger over self-inflicted harm comes from love. Any parent understands this emotion when they discover their child in a compromising environment. Therefore, see God's anger as an invitation to His love, not rejection just because you broke the rules. Be glad that He cares so much for your well being that He engages emotionally. God's wrath is real. It is a warning of what lies ahead. His anger is for our protection.

Secondly, see the anger of loved ones as evidence of something gone wrong. Do not write off the emotional outburst of another as someone who has no self-control. Anger is a safety valve for everyone's well being. It allows us to 'blow off steam' when we feel slighted or insignificant. Be grateful when those who love you confront you. Your pride will take offense, but your humility will be teachable. Their anger may go somewhat over the top, but honor them still. Listen to criticism and see it as your accountability. Develop a heart of a child, the mind of a student and the hide of a rhinoceros. Invite confrontation. When you do, you will encounter anger. Better to deal with anger on your terms of endearment than on their terms of engagement. Anger from people who care is meant to be redemptive and not destructive. Constructive anger respects the person, but rejects bad behavior. The anger of Jesus was not passive aggressive. He was expressive (John 2:15).

Therefore, be grateful that God gets mad. It is wise to fear His reactions to our unwise actions. Flee from foolish habits. If you have to sneak around to do something, it should tell you something. Can you imagine where we might be without the fear of God throttling back our behavior? See God's anger from the lens of love. It is warm acceptance of you, and cold rejection of sinful attitudes and actions. Therefore, interpret anger as an opportunity to grow and change. See it as a wake up call from Christ!

REFLECTIONS

_____

_____

_____

_____

_____

_____

57

PROVIDENCE PROMOTES

No one from the east or the west or from the desert can exalt a man.
But it is God who judges: He brings down one, he exalts another.
Psalm 75:6-7

Sometimes we strive unnecessarily in seeking promotion. We forget that heaven's hand handles this responsibility. Joseph discovered this when he went from the pit of death to the palace of power (Genesis 39). This doesn't lessen our commitment to excellence, but it does cause us to lean hard into the Lord. He is our promoter. He is our agent for advancement. Respected athletes and authors understand their dependence on professionals to place them in front of the right people at the right time. They hire agents and promoters to advance their careers. However in Christ, Almighty God advances our careers. He is our advance man. He is networked, because He created the network. Do not overlook the obvious. Allow Providence to be your promoter. Things do not occur by happen stance. The timing of your advancement is ordained in heaven not on earth.

Therefore, pray to your promoter Jesus. Talk with Him about His role and your responsibility. Like the owner who gave responsibility to three managers while he was away, God does have expectations for your part (Matthew 25). The providence of God does not mean you are passive. It means you are prayerfully engaged in His activities. You are faithful in following your Heavenly Father's agenda. Furthermore, be careful not to complicate the promotional process. It is all about stewarding wisely your relationships, money and time. It is doing excellent work with the motive of glorifying God. Focus on giving Him credit for your accomplishments, and He may entrust you with more responsibility. Performance is important, but it is performance lead by Providence. The quality of your work and relationships is a reflection on Jesus. He looks for those He can lift up who represent Him well. Providence promotes selfless people (Luke 14:11).

Yes there will others who manipulate their way into more prestigious roles. But do not follow their selfish shortcuts. It is not about who advances the fastest. A premature promotion can be perilous. Some who arrive too soon are sent back to the beginning. Indeed, promotions stick when your Savior is the instigator. Bosses are puppets in the hand of Providence. God can change their hearts, or change their role to carry out His ways. Therefore, use this parenthesis of time before you are promoted to prepare your character. New responsibilities require more intense integrity and a deep reservoir of faith. Stay focused on faith development and leave the opening and closing of doors to divine discretion. Let the Lord bring opportunity beckoning.

Above all else, do not miss Him in the middle of your motivation for advancement. He will give you the people, passion and provisions for your new role. Moses had Aaron. Jesus had Peter, James and John. Paul had Silas, Timothy and Barnabas. Martha had Mary. Indeed, serve people, so they will serve Him. Love people, so they will love Him. Value what God values, and there is a good chance others will do the same. The purpose for promotion is for Providence. It is a platform to love people for the Lord. It is a place where God's influence intersects people's lives. Moreover, give Christ credit and He will give you calm. Peace precedes Providence's promotion!

REFLECTIONS

_____

_____

_____

_____

_____

_____

58

REFLECTION OF GOD

You are resplendent with light, more majestic than mountains rich with game.
Psalm 76:4

Followers of Jesus are a reflection of Jesus. This is who we are. Just as the moon is a reflection of the sun, we are a reflection of the Son. God's son shines through our soul and breaks out into our behavior. His beam of light blankets our life like the sun's reflective rays on a sunbather exposed to a hot summer day. Indeed, God created light (Genesis 1:3). He is our Lord and the Lord of light. He invites us to walk in the greater light of His love and not the lesser light of our lust. The light of His love longs to lead us into a portrait of His character. His passion is for us to be poster children of His grace. So focus on being like Jesus and don't be driven by doing for Jesus. People are drawn to a life that reflects the Lord. A reflector needs only to be in an optimal position to reflect.

Indeed, it is when we are in right relationship with our Heavenly Father that we are right for reflection. All hindrances to dull lighting are destroyed when we deem it necessary to stay surrendered to our Savior. He lights up a life that is submitted to Him. The lampshade of sin is removed when we confess to Christ our desperate dependence on Him. He handles our influence and effectiveness as we are positioned properly in Him. Because we are in Christ, we are in the light. We shine because our Savior shines through us, and His bountiful beams of light bounce off of our beautiful behavior. Light is translucent. It reflects best off holiness. Character ignites the light of the Lord to reach into the darkest crevices of our world. You are the light of the Lord (Ephesians 5:8).

When we forgive, we reflect Jesus. When we care, we reflect Christ. When we cry over the condition of Christ-less souls, we reflect what our Lord experienced when He wept over the lost condition of His people (Luke 19:41-42). When we feed the hungry, cloth the naked, administer medical care to the sick, and house the homeless, we reflect Jesus. When we speak a word of encouragement, we reflect Christ. When we are kind instead of cross, we reflect Christ on the cross. When we give generously, we reflect God. When we build hospitals, schools, churches, and provide clean water, we reflect the Lord. When we are honest, kind, selfless, patient, loving, and a good listener, we reflect the Lord. When we are accountable and enforce accountability, we reflect Almighty God. When we take the time to lovingly speak truth, we reflect the Lord. When we fulfill our commitments, we reflect Christ. Reflecting God means we resolve to be who we are in Christ.

Lastly, lead others into the light of the Lord. Use your home to illuminate His love. Your home can become a little bit of heaven to those whose lives are a lot like hell. Invest time and money in those who cannot or will not give back. Orphans, single parents, the jobless, the homeless, homosexuals, adulterers, divorcees and the poor all need the warmth of God's love. Some find themselves in a Christ-less condition. They are cold and needy. They may feel God has forsaken them in their dark and depressed state. Thus, reflect God to them. Be a responsible citizen in the Kingdom of light (Colossians 1:12)!

REFLECTIONS

_____

_____

_____

_____

_____

_____

59

A GOOD MEMORY

I will remember the good deeds of the Lord;
yes, I will remember your miracles of long ago.
I will meditate on all your works and consider all your mighty deeds.
Psalm 77:11-12

A good memory makes for a faithful follower of Jesus. It is good when our soul flies back and reflects on His faithfulness. It is when we become shortsighted in our faith that we struggle and become stressed out. Our memory is a fit mercenary for faith. Good memories remind us of the goodness of God. His track record can be trusted. You may be experiencing a famine of faith, but you can still draw on the storehouse of stories that illustrate the past works of God. Release today's troubles into oblivion; cling instead to the marvelous deeds of the Lord that cannot be forgotten. Faith is a considering grace. It grows grander with time and grateful reflection. Indeed, beware of short-term memory loss in your trust of the Lord. Even Jesus' disciples wrestled with this (Matthew 16:9).

A good memory brings back to remembrance God's good deeds. Remember when He redirected your life from a disastrous outcome to one filled with peace and hope. See the branding of His love that is burned within the soft spot of your soul. He bought you with the price of His precious son Jesus. You are no longer your own, but you are His. This is a majestic memory of switching masters. Now your allegiance is to Almighty God. Your memory may bring back prayers He has answered, people who have come to Christ, children who have been born, or conversations with other Christ followers. You see some memories captured in photos, forever framed and not forgotten. Moreover, go back often to the Scripture He has seared in your mind as a memory of His promises. Jesus said to remember His words (John 15:20). His words woo us back when we wander away.

It is the art of meditation that brings back good memories. Meditation makes rich talking. However, unused thinking freezes up faith. Like dilapidated machinery that is over run with rust, so is a mind that does not meditate. Conversations without contemplation are barren of substance. Meditation makes for more meaningful talk. Therefore, do not depend on others to do your thinking for you. Meditation is meant for you. It hones your heart and sharpens your soul. A meditative man or woman should not be shy to share their musings; otherwise they are mental misers. Once you have been with Jesus, share your pearls of insight with other interested souls. Write out what He says so you can filter your thinking into pure words and phrases not to be easily forgotten.

Lastly, avoid filling your mind with useless information. Use the same discipline you employ in engaging truth with dispensing lies. Do not replay in your mind regrets and wishful thinking. What's done is done; nothing can change what has happened. Obsession with bad memories builds bitterness and betrays your freedom in Christ. Therefore, forget your former life of pain and focus on what you have gained with God. Forget your former life of unprincipled living and embrace your new life in Christ (Galatians 4:7-9). By God's grace make new memories with Him!

REFLECTIONS

_____

_____

_____

_____

_____

_____

60

LISTEN TO LEARN

O my people, hear my teaching; listen to the words of my mouth.
Psalm 78:1

Students of Jesus listen to learn. They listen to Him and they listen to those He brings into their lives. Listening for the motivation of learning is meant to lead us closer to the Lord and others. This is why we 'give ear' to what He says. We give earnest attention to hear the Almighty and act on His words. Obedience is a sign of effective listening. If God says one thing and we do another, we are either poor listeners or openly rebellious. Wise is the man or woman who listens well to the Lord. What He has to say is of great substance. Sometimes He extends His truth on the tongues of Bible teachers, other times He speaks quietly through His creation, or loudly through a loved one. However He speaks, we are to lean forward with our life into a listening posture. Jesus spoke as one with authority and people listened (Matthew 7:28-29). Wisdom listens and learns.

We give our undivided attention to University teachers so we can earn a degree and make a living. We listen to and appreciate the harmony and melody of majestic music. It frees our soul and lifts our spirits. We listen to an officer of the law when he writes us a speeding ticket and admonishes us to slow down. Indeed, the habit of not listening can get us into trouble. But there is a deeper level of listening that engages our heart around eternal issues. It focuses on the principles of Providence for the purpose of making a life. Listening to learn is motivated to harmonize the gospels and understand the context of Christ's teaching. Jesus said, 'learn from me...'(Matthew 11:29). A first step in learning to listen is obeying. Because He learned obedience, so can we (Hebrews 5:8).

Furthermore, it is not enough just to listen and learn from the Lord. Our listening and learning extends to people. It keeps eye contact with people and does not drift away. It is body language that oozes in respect and responsiveness. God has a lesson for us to learn with almost everyone we come into contact. But we will miss His instruction if we do not intently 'listen to learn' from others. We show love to others when we listen to them. They feel valued and affirmed. What really engages and energizes them is when we act on their ideas and suggestions. Wisdom values the instruction of everyone. Listen to others with the same undivided attention you give to God. Therefore, do not be slow to learn (Hebrews 5:11) because of poor listening skills. Slow down your spirit and focus in the moment. Repeat back what you think you heard, so you have clear comprehension with an eye to application. Listening to learn does not mean acquiescing to all admonishment, but it does mean prayerfully taking to heart what you hear.

Lastly, once you have listened and learned, pass on your valuable lessons to others. The best teachers are excellent listeners. Effective teachers engage hearts and minds. They do not just transfer information. Transformation is the outcome of their teaching. Teachers who listen well are much better prepared to teach well. You pass on your 'learning from listening' to those who are eager to listen and learn. Therefore, listen and you will learn more easily. Do not listen, and learning is hard. Learn to listen and you will learn!

REFLECTIONS

_____

_____

_____

_____

_____

_____

61

SUFFERING AND SEEKING

Whenever God slew them, they would seek him;
they eagerly turned to him again.
Psalm 78:34

Suffering has the tendency to shake us into seeking the Lord. It is when we become uncomfortable in our circumstances that we long for the Lord. Christ becomes our interest when our interests are interrupted. It is not a bad thing when suffering sends us to our Savior. Furthermore, we tend to get comfortable with Christ when everything goes our way. Our faith can become too familiar when we take our Heavenly Father for granted. And then life happens and God allows all hell to break loose in our home. It may be a spouse who begins to flirt with sin and falls into temptation's trap. However, marriage blow-ups are meant to bring us back to God. It is not that we didn't know Him before our world was rocked. We knew Him in our salvation, but we didn't know Him in our suffering. Suffering moves us beyond the surface with our Savior to an intense level of loving intimacy and dependency. It is in the moments of our sufferings that we come to understand what it is like to share with Him in His sufferings (Philippians 3:10).

We tend to obey when we resonate with the rod of God's reprove. He disciplines us when we get out of line (Hebrews 12:5-11). Because He loves us He longs for us to seek Him with all our heart. Sincere seeking of the Lord is not half-hearted, but hot-hearted. It is a passionate desire for unhindered intimacy. Moreover, spiritually dead hearts need a robust charge from Christ. Like a heart attack victim in the emergency room needs the paddles of an electrical charge, so a sin soiled and stubborn heart needs the shock of suffering to awaken it to Almighty God. Ironically our suffering is for us to get our eyes off ourselves and on to Him. Suffering delivers us from ourselves to God. It is in our suffering that we see Christ clearly. Don't pity yourself by staying stuck on yourself, but propel yourself by faith into the arms of your Heavenly Father. He loves you.

He does mean for us to move toward piety when we are plagued from within and without. By faith we cast our inward burdens on Him, when outward burdens continue to press down hard on our life. The sharp strokes of suffering awaken the memories of God's faithfulness. Reflection follows inflection. When our props of pride are knocked away, we are positioned for total dependence on the Lord. Maybe your career has gone south, then go hard after Him. Maybe you have become soft on sin, then go hard after Him. Maybe you have been treated unfairly, then go hard after Him. Maybe your anger has the best of you, then go hard after Him. Maybe you are bankrupted financially and figuratively, then go hard after Him. Use this time of suffering to seek your Savior.

Lastly, suffering from the Lord's discipline is for our good that we may share in His holiness (Hebrews 12:10). It is painful for now, but will produce a harvest of righteousness. Holiness means He has all of you. Indeed, teach your children what to do and what not to do. Let them learn from your mistakes. Leverage your sufferings for their sakes. See God in your suffering. Do not stay mad. Move toward God and be glad!

REFLECTIONS

_____

_____

_____

_____

_____

_____

62

PRODIGAL FATHERS

How often they rebelled against him in the desert and grieved him
in the wasteland! Again and again they put God to the test;
they vexed the Holy One of Israel…
Psalm 78:40-41

Prodigal fathers penetrate our society like a blunted rusty nail through a soft shoe. They are painful and poisonous. Pride drives them into irrational thinking and erratic behavior. Why do some fathers run away from their responsibilities of a husband and a dad? A simple answer is selfishness. A more complex reason is no fear of God and no regard for right and wrong. Men left to their own devices can justify anything, even in the name of religion. A man does not leave his family without first leaving God. Prodigal dads are as constant in provocation of Providence as He is in extending patience toward them. It is rebellion against the Almighty that jettisons a man's faith. It may be a quiet and passive aggressive rebellion, or it may be an all out kicking and screaming rebellion. The tragic results are all the same. Foolish is the man who pursues fun over faith and family.

Prodigals want the benefits of being a man with the responsibilities of being a boy. Some men spend a lifetime making excuses for not maturing. Why? It may be a hurt that has never healed. Wounded men wound others. Wounds without the balm of belief in God's grace never go away. They may drive you to run away, but they stay. Wounds build walls between relationships. They are a hindrance to happiness and holiness. Prodigal fathers are also angry. Their unresolved and conflicting emotions make them mad. They are mad at God for not fixing them. They are mad at their family for not seeming to care. And they are mad at them-selves for not being honest about their struggles. It is in his desert of desperation that a man takes flight in his faith, or he takes refuge in God. Do not allow your desert to become a wilderness by deserting God. Sin is not worth the effect of grieving God. Instead turn back to your loving Heavenly Father. He'll make you a man.

Furthermore, if you are the recipient of a prodigal father's irresponsible action you have hope. You have a Heavenly Father who cannot be tempted by evil (James 1:13). Your Heavenly Father is there for you to love on you, and to lead you into a deeper love relationship. Use this time of rejection to be accepted in the Beloved (Ephesians 1:6 KJV). Almighty God is never AWOL (absent without official leave) in His love relationship with you. You do not have to worry or wonder if He is there for you. He is always by your side. Not only is He with you, He wants to serve you. God is a giver. He is a Heavenly Father who cares so much that He has at His disposal heaven's resources just for you. Love? You have it. Wisdom? It's yours. Encouragement? Every day!

Lastly, pray about pursuing your prodigal father. Your presence reminds him of what God has for him. Christ in your life convicts him of who he needs to be, and what he needs to do. Inside your prodigal father is like a scared and wounded animal in need of a gentle touch and healing. It is the Holy Spirit's work, through you and other believers, that will bring him to his knees. Be there for him, because one day he will need you and God. Keep the relationship robust for when he returns home. Your forgiveness fuels his faith!

REFLECTIONS

_____

_____

_____

_____

_____

_____

63

EMPOWERING LEADERSHIP

And David shepherded them with integrity of heart;
and with skillful hands he lead them.
Psalm 78:72

Leadership can be daunting and even overwhelming. But it is when a leader lacks that he needs to exhibit integrity. He may lack experience in new area, so he admits his shortcomings and is open and honest about his need for the expertise of the team. If he tries to mask his mistakes he will only muddle along, while maintaining at best. Eventually, his inabilities will come out. It is better to release our inexperience upfront than to hide, or ignore it until it explodes forth on its own. Leaders of integrity know what they can and cannot do well. They look to others to shore up their weakness, and they serve others out of their strengths. Numbers may not be your thing, however you can learn to read a balance sheet and profit/loss report. Make sure in your leadership you are always learning about things that are uncomfortable for you. You can be educated without having to become an expert. Indeed, integrity becomes a student of asking.

Leaders who empower lead out of a position of humility. This means they have more questions than answers. They help other team members discover the best answers. They lead a conversation of questioning. The leader is not the guru with all knowledge. They are the CQA (Chief Question Asker). Empowering leaders engage the mind of other team members. They are skilled at harvesting the outstanding thinking of everyone and converging it into the best answer. This is difficult for hard driving leaders who want to get to the bottom line as quick as possible and execute. The direct approach gets results sooner, but lacks sustainability. Better to go through a process of debate and buy in, and thus guarantee a galvanized commitment from everyone. Skilled leaders understand how to encourage everyone to think, create solutions and implement thoroughly. It is easier and somewhat more efficient to think for others. However, though it takes longer and requires more patience and emotional intelligence, empowering leadership is the most effective. Collective thinking from the whole lasts much longer.

Therefore, ask God for wisdom to understand what questions to ask, and the patience to not answer before others have the time to process. It is in our waiting that God makes leaders out of followers. Followers who fail to think stay stunted in their leadership. They are limited leaders. However, followers who learn to think grow their leadership capacity. They can eventually surpass their leader's leadership. This is what you want. You want to work yourself out of a job, so you in turn can grow your leadership capacity, while engaging in other options that are best for you and the organization. Patience and wise leaders grow a team that surpasses them.

Lastly, skilled leaders are able to discern those who do not have the capability to grow as leaders. Maybe they do not have leadership DNA within them. Or, they may not have the character to handle the demands of leadership. Expel team members of bad character or they will corrupt the whole. Their bad motives may be as obvious and loud as a rattlesnake, or they may be quiet and deceptive as a water moccasin, either way they are dangerous and can be lethal. Do not tolerate troublemakers. On the other hand some team members may have the character, but not the competence to grow into leaders. Make sure they understand this and position them properly. Skilled leaders of integrity value everyone. They lead others to think and they develop followers into leaders. Above all else, they look to the Lord's leadership. This is empowering leadership!

REFLECTIONS

_____

_____

_____

_____

_____

_____

64

DESPERATE NEED

may your mercy come quickly to meet us, for we are in desperate need.
Help us, O God our Savior…
Psalm 79:8b-9a

Everyone is in desperate need of God. There are no exemptions. The rich desperately need God. The poor desperately need God. The intelligent desperately need God. The dumb desperately need God. The educated desperately need God. The ignorant desperately need God. The respected desperately need God. The disrespected desperately need God. The wise desperately need God. The foolish desperately need God. No one can honestly dismiss his or her desperate need for God. We are all men or women in desperate need of God our Savior. We quietly lead needy lives, not because we are without hope. We are desperately needy because we cannot save ourselves. In and of ourselves we have no hope. Our desperation graduates to despair if we stay there.

However, in Christ we have a living hope that meets our every need. Paul states it well, "And my God will meet all your needs according to his glorious riches in Christ Jesus (Philippians 4:19). But it is only when we acknowledge our desperate need for Christ that we are ready to receive His grace. The non-needy think they have no need for God. Unfortunately, for some it takes a crisis to awaken them to their desperate need for Christ. They slumber away in their sin-sedated state, only tipping God with trivial pursuit, while their real passions in life are driven by pride, money, sex, or power. Or, they find fulfillment in other respected places like family, work or community service, all of which in and of themselves serve a very good purpose. But, our interests however narcissistic or noble cannot substitute for our desperate need for God's goodness and mercy to lead our lives, and manage our motives. It is in our desperate need for God that we gain perspective.

The compelling truth is, because of our desperate need for Christ we can rejoice (Isaiah 29:19). We are full of joy because we know Jesus is our Savior and Lord. Because our redeemer lives, we can face tomorrow. Your desperate need leads you to the Lord. This is where you find peace and patience. Sin loses its allure when you cling to Christ. Your teach-ability and trust rise in an environment of desperate need. You would not need God, if you were not needy for God. Furthermore, self-sufficiency will try to slither its way into you thinking as you experience success. However, your success translates into a greater need for God. Without utter abandonment to Almighty God success will suck you into Kingdom irrelevance.

Therefore, because we are all desperately needy for God, there is no room for pride. We are all beggars who have the opportunity to share the bread of God's grace with each other and with outsiders. It is in the humility of our needy condition that we have the opportunity to model dependency and total trust. We are sheep in need of a shepherd. With Him we look smart and confident. Without Him we look confused and lost. It is one of the many paradoxes of following Jesus. Desperate dependence on Christ within, leads to a quiet confidence without. When you die, you live. When you give up, you win. When you surrender, you are victorious. When you give, you receive. When you are desperately needy, you become radically restored. Fulfillment comes by faith in Him!

REFLECTIONS

_____

_____

_____

_____

_____

_____

65

NEW OPPORTUNITY

You brought a vine out of Egypt; you drove out the nations and planted it.
You cleared the ground for it, and it took root and filled the land.
Psalm 80:8-9

Sometimes we need a new opportunity. We need it to challenge our career path. We need it to further our faith. We need it to nurture the soil of our soul. God knows this. He knows our need to conquer new goals and grow closer to Him. The soil of your situation may be fallow and fruitless. It seems like everyone is on a different page and there is no strategic direction. The vision is unclear and the mission is muddled. You have remained faithful during the downturn, but now circumstances have somewhat stabilized. You may be like a star athlete who has performed well for a season, but the chemistry has changed. A trade to a different team is what is best for everyone. It is the time to transition. Transition requires trust. A new opportunity requires you to ratchet up your faith in your Heavenly Father. Celebrate what Christ has done through you and move on by faith.

Many times you are called to a new opportunity because of wise stewardship. You have managed well what God has given you, and now He is opening up another door of opportunity. Your attention to detail and ability to lead people into excellence has not gone unnoticed. God has nurtured your life like a small vine, and has prepared it to be vibrant and healthy. He is poised to multiply your efforts exponentially for His eternal purposes. God has cared for you, so you can care for others. Healthy vines produce firm branches with luscious fruit. God wants to plant you in this new opportunity because the soil is fertile and moist. He has prepared this next season for your roots to go deep and wide for the Kingdom of God. His tender transplanting will yield mountains of fruit.

However, do not allow this change to challenge your relationship with Christ. In this new opportunity you will need Him as much if not more than in your past productivity. There may very well be more resources and better-equipped people, but you still need your Savior in spades. New opportunity is sometimes necessary to shake us out of our comfort zone, and cause us to cling to Christ. If we are not careful, we drift into mediocrity, and just mess around with what God has given us. A new opportunity gives us a fresh appreciation and motivation. So seek this new opportunity prayerfully. It may be a new church. It may be a new job. It may be a new boyfriend or girlfriend. It may be a new hobby. It may be a new move across the world. It may a new investment. It may be a new and smaller house.

Receive whatever new opportunity awaits you by faith, and do not look back. Lot's wife turned to salt when she looked back on her old life with regret (Genesis 19:26). Israel stayed confused when they looked back and second-guessed their exodus from Egypt (Numbers 14:3-4). Stay focused ahead on what Almighty God has for you next. When you signed up for Jesus as your Savior, it was an automatic 'yes' to your next assignment, before you even knew the details. Indeed, a new opportunity, accompanied by the Lord, is next to heaven. Out on the limb with Jesus is the location of the best fruit. Steward it well and He will expand His influence through you. With Him you can do His next thing!

REFLECTIONS

_____

_____

_____

_____

_____

_____

66

LISTEN WELL

Hear, O my people, and I will warn you—
if you would but listen to me, O Israel!
Psalm 81:8

Sometimes we only listen to what we want to hear. Our listening becomes selective. Indeed, the worst type of lazy listening discriminates against the Almighty's voice. If we drift into this insensible state we become deaf to God. Maybe this is happening to you. Christ commands are falling on deaf ears. The sign language of your Savior is signaling you back to His holiness, His love and His care. Jesus taught the wisdom of listening to God. He said in John 6:46, "It is written in the Prophets: 'They will all be taught by God.' Everyone who listens to the Father and learns from him comes to me". It is in your educational exchange with eternity that you draw closer to Christ. He is your teacher.

Furthermore, listening lures us to the Lord. Like well positioned and attractive bait in front of a flirtatious fish, our Heavenly Father hooks us with truth. Often He uses godly messengers to get across His personalized message. John states it well, "We are from God, and whoever knows God listens to us; but whoever is not from God does not listen to us. This is how we recognize the Spirit of truth and the spirit of falsehood (1 John 4:6)." It is this active listening to the Almighty's ambassador's that we gain discernment into what to do, or what not to do. It is your spouse, your teacher, your parents, your pastor and your godly friends who speak on behalf of your Savior. Other vague voices may be louder and more persuasive, but do not succumb to their proud plea. Listen instead to those who you know love you, who you know want God's best for you. Listen well to their warnings.

Moreover, if you continue down the road of resistance to radical listening, then God may give you over to your desires. He doesn't waste His time with those who won't listen. He doesn't cast the pearls of His wisdom among stubborn swine (Matthew 7:6, KJV). He shares with those who steward well their listening. The Lord longs to engage your heart through the stability of Scripture. His Word screams truth. Nonetheless, avoid reacting to the last lingering voice you encounter. Instead, listen well in your encounters with Christ. Listen well to His pensive and pure voice through those who represent Him. Selective listening is smart when it defaults to Deity. Turn down the volume on the Christ-less culture which carelessly, but confidently, cries out for conformation to its creeds. There is only one voice that demands your undivided attention, Almighty God's. Therefore, be selective by listening well to what your Savior says. His words are what matter most!

REFLECTIONS

_____

_____

_____

_____

_____

_____

67

GOD PRESIDES

God presides in the great assembly; he gives judgment among the "gods."
Psalm 82:1

God presides over the courtroom of our culture. He is the Chief Justice over our cares, concerns and corruption. Nothing done in this life sneaks by our Savior. We can be certain that Christ will judge our actions, or our inactions. He is the judge to be feared. He is the judge our judges should fear. Moses sat in judgment of the people. They stood to plead their case and he sat, listened and dispensed wisdom (Exodus 18:13).

God was his model of justice. Indeed, the judges of our land are not the final answer. They answer to Almighty God. Woe to them if they acquit the guilty, or condemn the innocent. Great responsibility resides with the one who presides in judgment. Whatever the cause before them is God's cause. Therefore, pray for our judges to petition heaven for help.

There is a guide for defining right and wrong. The Bible is the basis for our justice system. Holy Scripture is the baseline for our laws. It defines and illustrates God's moral law. It is designed to be the conscious of our culture. Judges do have boundaries to prevent them from perverting justice. The same applies for us when we find ourselves in a position to preside over another's problems.

Two parties may bring to you conflicting opinions. Your first question as mediator is "What does the Bible teach?" "What eternal principles apply to this situation?" A child may be right in their grievance against their parents, but are they honoring them in the process (Ephesians 6:4). Use your level of influence to leverage what the Lord thinks. Engage conflict with Christ's perspective.

Lastly, live your life with actions that can stand under the scrutiny of your Savior. Be ever aware of the courtroom of Christ as your ultimate accountability (I Corinthians 3:11-13). What you do in the dark, where no one is watching, will one day come out under the light of the Lord (I Corinthians 4:5).

You may mask your motives with a smile and sincerity, but your true intent will one day be exposed. Moreover, others may be taking advantage of your good intentions. Trust them with God. He will judge them justly in His right timing. God presides over your position at work and home. Therefore, submit to Him and His ways. Live accountable to God. Prepare for your audit from the Almighty!

REFLECTIONS

_____

_____

_____

_____

_____

_____

68

SHAMED INTO SEEKING

Cover their faces with shame so that men will seek your name, O Lord.
Psalm 83:16

Shame can be a catalyst for seeking Christ. It is in our shame that we are positioned to seek the Lord. Our shameful state opens the door to our Savior Jesus. It is an advocate who gains us an audience with the Almighty. Therefore, do not stay shamed. You may have been caught stealing, lying or flirting with another person's spouse. Your drinking may have become excessive, or your prescription drugs lingered too long. Your gossip got the best of you. The state of your mind, soul and body is sick and ashamed. Your irresponsible actions have come to light. You are embarrassed. But, you can be relieved that your shameful indiscretions can give you a new lease with the Lord. Shame is meant to wean us from our idols, and set us on the path of pursuing Christ. It is in our most embarrassing moments that we need to remember the love and acceptance of our Heavenly Father. Like the prodigal son who became ashamed of his sin, came to his senses, and sought forgiveness from the one he had sinned against (Luke 15:17).

Once God has covered your face in shame, you can uncover it by seeking the forgiveness of Christ. There is no level of shameful sin that He cannot cleanse. It is when we think we have gone too far that we fear fostering faith. However, in this life you cannot go beyond the grace of God, no matter the significance of your shame. So, seek Christ while He can be found. You may be ashamed for not appropriating His grace sooner, but you will not be ashamed for calling on His name now. Speak the name of Jesus. It sooths your shame and satisfies your soul. His name is wonderful. His name is beautiful. His name is above every name, and it is at His name that you will one-day bow in unfettered and shameless worship (Philippians 2:9-11). The glorious name of Jehovah was spoken by the Jews. The precious name of Jesus is forever on the lips of those who love the Lord. Mention the name of Jesus and experience His good graces. His name is nourishment for your soul.

Therefore, awaken from your shameful slumber. The constant correction in your conscience is Christ. He loves you too much to leave you in your shameful state. Renew your mind from any temporary amnesia to the Almighty's ways of doing things (Romans 12:1-2). This world likes to keep you in the dark. It will gently rock you to sleep in the cradle of its cravings. Shameful and alarming are the ways of the world. But, peaceful and content are the ways of God. So, do not be ashamed to seek the Lord. Shame is a wake up call to the callousness of sin, and the caressing care of Christ. Be glad that you feel shame when you sin. It reminds you of the need for your Savior. It is God's way of getting your attention. It is better to suffer a little shame now than to shutter the thought of a shameful judgment day. Seek Him while He may be found. Seek Him now while it really matters. Be ever present in prayerful petition. Shame is His means to seeking Him!

REFLECTIONS

_____

_____

_____

_____

_____

_____

69

GOD'S GATEKEEPER

Better is one day in your courts than a thousand elsewhere;
I would rather be a doorkeeper in the house of my God
than dwell in the tents of the wicked.
Psalm 84:10

We are God's gatekeepers. We are the gatekeepers of His truth. We are the gatekeepers of His trust. We are the gatekeepers of His time. We are the gatekeepers of His grace. A gatekeeper for God is larger than life. It is better to have a lowly position with the Lord than a glamorous role without Him. A gatekeeper gets to see what's inside. We get a glimpse of God. We get to brush up against the Almighty.

Indeed, Jesus is our gate to God. This is how He described Himself, "I am the gate; whoever enters through me will be saved..." (John 10:9a). He is our passageway away from pride's grip into the humble hands of heaven. He is our threshold of trust. By God's grace we get to go there.

Moreover, a day as God's gatekeeper is more valuable and interesting than a thousand days somewhere intriguing, but much less significant. You can travel around the world in 80 days, but in one day, through prayer, you can make a pilgrimage to heaven. The tents of the wicked are adventurous and inviting, but in the end they are at the mercy of the world's elements. They are exposed to evil. The tents of the wicked travel like nomads.

They have no eternal destination in mind. It is all about surviving another day. They roam around in search of significance. However, the house of the Lord is full of hope. It is stable and dependable. The pillars of God's character rest on the foundation of His faithfulness. His house is forever accessible by faith. Jesus did not have an earthly home to lay His head (Luke 9:58), but He had a heavenly home to rest His heart.

Therefore, relish the opportunity to be God's gatekeeper. Show up to serve and see what He has in store. God's worst is better than the devil's best. There may be times you feel like the Lord has gone away. Like the entrepreneur who left town on business, and who left his stewards to manage his money resourcefully (Matthew 25:14ff). You may assume He has no need for your services, but He does, so remain faithful. Sometimes it is when you least expect it that the Lord lays on you a tremendous blessing.

But you have to believe, and be there to receive. Gatekeepers do not get the glory, but they observe glory. Your glimpse of God way supersedes your stare at sin. Your gate keeping gives you access to intimacy and wisdom. Enjoy your private conferences with Christ. Parley with Him in prayer. It is here that you hear your Heavenly Father's voice. Children crave their father's verbal affirmation. You are loved when Jesus speaks your name. Stay near to God's gate and you will experience Him. You get to God as His gatekeeper!

REFLECTIONS

_____

_____

_____

_____

_____

_____

70

PEACE PROMISE

I will listen to what the Lord will say; he promises peace to his people,
his saints—but let them not return to folly.
Psalm 85:8

God promises peace to his people. It is a peace produced in heaven and delivered on earth. God's peace provides us just what we need, not just to get through life, but also to excel in life. The peace of God propels us to go places we would have avoided, without the assurance of His peace. God's peace plan for His people is accessible at all times. It is when we forget to forge our faith around His plan that we forfeit peace.

God's process is to listen first, then act. Because God hears us, we are eager to hear Him. Hearing the voice of God vanquishes our fears and validates our peace. Grace waits to hear God, and then proceeds in peace. The disciples waited on the peace of Jesus. The Spirit engulfed them, then they preached, performed miracles and ministered to the people (John 20:21-23).

Moreover, God's peace proceeds from a heart of obedience. It is inaccessible to disobedience. Obstinacy to the ways of God does not gain the peace of God. It is when you make peace with God that you garner the grace and peace of God. Paul said it well; "Therefore, since we have been justified through faith, we have peace with God through our Lord Jesus Christ, through whom we have gained access by faith into this grace in which we now stand (Romans 5:1-2a)."

Peace is for the purposes of faith and not folly. Peace cannot be prostituted for personal gain. It is all about God and His game plan. We forgo peace when we go astray. We give up peace when we go our own way. However, if you find yourself in trouble, trust Him. His peace accompanies a humble and trusting heart. In the middle of your storm, listen to His voice say, "Peace, be still" (Mark 4:39 KJV). Calm comes with Christ. Joy comes from Jesus. The Lord gives lasting peace.

Lastly, let the Lord in on your peculiar predicament. He already knows and cares.

Confusion only continues when you try to work it out without Him. However, the peace of God does not require your total understanding. It transcends your troubled heart. It will guard your heart and mind in Christ Jesus (Philippians 4:7). Man's peace depends on treaties that can be broken. God's peace depends on your relationship with Jesus that cannot be broken. Man's peace is momentary.

God's peace is enduring. Listen to the voice of man and you may delay the peace process. Listen to the voice of God and you will accelerate the peace process. God provides peace to His children. His provision of His peace awaits your access. Therefore, pray and wait on His peace. His peace precludes fear. Listen intently to the Lord. His voice can be trusted. Appropriate His peace promise!

REFLECTIONS

_____

_____

_____

_____

_____

_____

UNDIVIDED HEART

Teach me your way, O Lord, and I will walk in your truth;
give me an undivided heart, that I may fear your name.
Psalm 86:11

An undivided heart unites around the will of God. The heart is headquarters for His purposes. It is here that humility reigns with focus and clarity, but pride's rule divides. The attributes of its scepter are awe and intimidation. Pride divides, while humility unites. It is our undivided devotion to God that determines our other devotions. It excludes some and creates others. So, as your faith becomes more focused, you become more focused. You do fewer things well, instead of many things mediocre.

Your life becomes a laser beam of implementation in the Lord's best. People may wonder why your efforts are increasingly intentional. You can tell them that God is teaching you to focus. Like an infant, you are growing beyond the milk of your salvation to the meat of His Word. Hebrews 6:1a teaches, "Therefore let us leave the elementary teachings about Christ and go on to maturity...".

So, an undivided heart is a student of the Lord's for life. There is no 'arriving' in this life. We don't know it all until we are in the presence of the Almighty. Indeed, the wise remain learners of the Lord's teachings. An undivided heart craves teaching that goes beyond the surface of salvation to the depths of dependence on God. The mature understanding of God gets to the heart of the matter. It is in this place of integrity where you divide your heart in disobedience, or unite it in obedience. An undivided heart places you on a path marked by His truth. It is walking in His ways.

Walking is a lifestyle. It is a way of doing things. Obedience to God's truth becomes a habit of doing life with an undivided heart. Your undivided heart propels you along His prayerful and proper path. He walks with you in the valley of death (Psalm 23:4) and on the mountaintop of life (Matthew 17:1-3). A faith focused heart invites your Heavenly Father in. It is a fulcrum for your faith.

Therefore, avoid double minded duties. God hates double-mindedness (Psalm 119:113). Only when you draw near to God can you deal with double-mindedness (James 4:8). Double-mindedness is a first cousin of a divided heart. Instead, unite around Christ and His teachings. Make His behavior the baseline for your life and work. It may mean engaging professional services that align more with your values.

It may mean changing to a church that unapologetically teaches God's Word. It may mean breaking off a relationship that divides your heart and conflicts your mind. A united heart does not avoid the difficult path of obedience. It submits to its Savior and models Him. Though you may be torn, make sure to trust by praying, "Not my will, but Your will be done"!

REFLECTIONS

_____

_____

_____

_____

_____

_____

72

FAITHFUL FOUNDATION

He has set his foundation on the holy mountain.
Psalm 87:1

Your Heavenly Father provides a faithful foundation. He provides it in your personal faith. He provides it for your church. And He provides it in your relationships. When you placed your faith in Christ you established your values and beliefs on the Rock of Ages. Jesus Christ is your foundation for religious commitment. Your commitment to the church flows out of your commitment to Christ.

Personal faith is foundational for the character of Christ to transform your life. It is this foundation of faith that is forever yours. No amount of adversity or acclaim can remove His faithful foundation of holiness, humility, forgiveness, courage and perseverance. Dismay dissolves when you place your trust in Christ. He is the cornerstone of your Sovereign Lord's foundation (Isaiah 28:16).

The church is established and built on the faithful foundation of your Heavenly Father. God's household is built on the foundation of the apostles and prophets with Christ as the chief cornerstone. In Him the whole building rises up to become His holy place of worship (Ephesians 2:19-21). The church of the living God is the pillar and foundation of truth. It is here that God's household gets a handle on how to conduct their lives (I Timothy 3:15).

However, the church is only effective as it implements its operational manual, the Bible. The church can only define truth as it is taught from holy writ. Full disclosure of God's writings invites the Holy Spirit's application to humble hearts. Therefore, stay engaged in a church whose foundation is faith in Christ, and whose pillars are the proclamation of Scripture. Hell cannot prevail against the church (Matthew 16:18, KJV).

Lastly, God provides a faithful foundation to facilitate your relationships. His grace is the lubricant for love and forgiveness. His power and confidence is what gives you the courage to confront with conduct that is becoming to Christ. Relationships built on Christ persevere. They last because the Lord lasts. When Christ is your reason for the relationship then you seek to out to serve others. What they need and want becomes primary.

You are devoted to one another and you honor one another above yourselves (Romans 12:10). This level of relational unselfishness can only be founded on the Lord. Build on His foundation and lay up for yourselves eternal rewards; you one day will return to worship at His feet (I Corinthians 3:10-15; Revelation 4:11). Your faith, your church and your relationships will flourish on God's faithful foundation. Become His bold builder!

REFLECTIONS

_____

_____

_____

_____

_____

_____

73

AFTER LIFE

Do you show your wonders to the dead?
Do those who are dead rise up and praise you?
Psalm 88:10

After life: is the Lord for those who love the Lord. After life: is Lordless for those who do not love the Lord. This is why it is imperative you get into right relationship with God in this life, so you don't get it wrong after life. Yes, there is more to look forward to than cold dirt for your cold body. Your body does turn back into the dust from which God's breathe created the first human flesh in Adam (Genesis 2:7).

But your body does not remain cold and rigid. There is an afterlife. The Bible teaches in I Thessalonians 4:15-17 that the dead in Christ shall rise first. Indeed, the same God who rose up His son Jesus will rise up His sons and daughters in the faith. Take heart, because there is a massive transformation that takes place after life. God is not done, until He gets it done.

Advance technology can prolong life, but it cannot resurrect life. No amount of discoveries will ever lead to what is only in the hands of heaven. No amount of medicine can make a man or woman live forever. However, death is not bad for believers in Jesus Christ. It is a bridge of belief to something much better. Indeed, your lamenting in this life becomes laughter in the next. Your mourning in this life becomes celebration in the next. Your worry in this life becomes worship in the next.

Your complaints in this life become gratitude in the next. The afterlife is all about Almighty God and His agenda. There is much more to come, because He is the God of the living. Jesus said, "But about the resurrection of the dead—have you not read what God said to you, 'I am the God of Abraham, the God of Isaac, and the God of Jacob'? He is not the God of the dead but of the living" (Matthew 22:31-32). You will follow your risen Savior after life.

Therefore, take hope and live as if you will one day rise from the dead. Life for those who love the Lord is not the deadend street of sin, but a bridge into paradise with Jesus (Luke 23:43). You have the promise of your personal resurrection. You have the proof of your Savior's resurrection. Men and women who reject the resurrection route trod down the path to hell (Luke 16:23).

Moreover, death or life without an afterlife is meaningless. But because you believe in an after life, this life is full of purpose and eternal rewards. This life is all about loving the Lord and loving people. This life is about dying to self and living for Him. This life is about gratitude and generosity, because of your gracious and gigantic God. The anticipation of an afterlife makes this life explode with meaning and hope. Be encouraged, you serve the God of the living... after life!

REFLECTIONS

_____

_____

_____

_____

_____

_____

74

SECRET SINS

You have set our iniquities before you, our secret sins
in the light of your presence.
Psalm 90:8

Secret sins do not remain a secret. They are always before Almighty God, and they eventually come to light to those who love and respect us. Secret sins are not a risk worth taking. There is no up side and a massive downside. Secret sins can seem harmless, but they are sinister in their intent, and deadly in their outcomes. There is nothing good that comes from secret sins. It leads to death. Death of life. Death of relationships. Death of vision.

Above all else, it is spiritual suicide. Secret sins grow into an animal that cannot be tamed. Even a godly man like David was not immune to its allure. He allowed power to fuel his secret sins of pride, lust, adultery and murder. But the consequences were beyond grief. In Psalm 51 you hear his body and soul reel from the results of sin.

Eventually, God's eternal light exposes sin. "God is light, in him is no darkness at all" (I John 1:5). There are no secret sins before God. No one can dupe the divine. He deals severely and justly with sin. However, He did provide His son Jesus as your Savior from secret sins. Without Jesus you cannot overcome sin's snare. Lust looks good, but then it drives you out of control. Sin does not play fair. It is dispassionate in its effect.

Like a parasite, pride sucks out the spiritual life from its host. It thinks it has everything under control, while all the while it spirals out of control. Paul said it well, "Be not deceived, God cannot be mocked. A man reaps what he sows" (Galatians 6:7). Therefore, invite friends into your secret sin. Share your secret. Admission creates a way out.

Moreover, fear God and you will fear sin. Fear of God fosters a healthy view of sin. The Lord loathes sin, but He forgives the sinner (I Thessalonians 2:16, I John

4:10). Secret sin is cancer to your soul. It clutters your conscience. However, in Christ you have been set free from sin and become a slave of God (Romans 6:22). The most effective remedy for secret sins is confession, repentance and accountability.

Tell your spouse if you are emotionally attracted to a work associate. Do not keep secrets from those who hold you accountable. Come out of the closet of compromise and come clean with Christ. Secluded sin gains control. Confessed sin loses control. Jesus died on the cross openly for your secret sin. Therefore, embrace His powerful public payment of your secret sin. Secret sin slithers away into irrelevance under the shadow of the cross. Don't keep it a secret!

REFLECTIONS

_____

_____

_____

_____

_____

_____

75

REST IN THE LORD

He who dwells in the shelter of the Most High
will rest in the shadow of the Almighty.
Psalm 91:1

The shadow of God is your shelter. He is your resting place. Furthermore, peace is a product of resting in God's care. The wicked forfeit this peace (Isaiah 57:21). The temptation is to only run to our Savior's shelter in times of trouble. This is not necessary. Instead, you can habitually hang out in God's inner sanctuary of intimacy.

Do not wait for hell to drive you to heaven. The Lord is not a last resort. He deserves and expects your full attention, real time. Consequently, you get to reside in the peaceful presence of Jesus. He said, "Peace I leave with you; my peace I give you...(John 14:27)".

The fruit of rest results when you remain in Christ (John 15:4). Rest is the residue of remaining in Him. It is when you are far off from fellowship with your Heavenly Father that you fret and find yourself fatigued. However, when you are governed by grace you obtain continual communion with Christ. Intimacy with Him offers rest.

Moreover, make sure you do not substitute your devotion to God with your service for God. You rest only when your 'Martha service' is motivated by your 'Mary devotion' (Luke 10:38-41). If not you become exhausted, ungrateful and discouraged. Rest results from resting in Him.

So, seek the shadow of the Almighty, during the noxious heat of everyday life. Take one lunch break a week just to be with the Lord. You may take a walk in the woods, or sit in the car and worship Him with uplifting music. Shut your office door and pray on your knees. Make your own canopy of Christ worship. Indeed, the shadow of the Almighty is your security against insecurity. It is your comfort during crisis. It is your salvation during sickness. It is your hope in the middle of a horrific event.

Therefore, take a deep breath of belief. You rest when you exhale worry and inhale trust. It is under His reassuring shadow that you see Him. Take your attention off your struggles and fears. Focus on Him. Face God first and then you are ready to face your fears. Your giants of fear become pygmies of peace when you rest under the influence of God's presence. Take shelter under His shadow. Get under the Almighty. This is your reoccurring rest!

REFLECTIONS

_____

_____

_____

_____

_____

_____

76

STAY FRESH

They will still bear fruit in old age, they will stay fresh and green.
Psalm 92:14

Stay fresh in your faith. Otherwise, you are set up to falter and not finish well. Fresh faith is compelling. It is clean and crisp like the beginning of a new day. However, be careful. The older you get, the more familiar your faith becomes. It is easy to lose your freshness. Your focus drifts to your ailments and away from Almighty God. Your faith grows stale and tasteless. But fresh faith is appetizing and inviting. It piques the interest of others. They smell the fumes of your faith and it is sweet to their senses.

Like a freshly lit scented candle, the aroma of your life puts off a soothing smell. You are spiritually attractive. Paul taught this, "But thanks be to God, who always leads us in triumphal procession in Christ and through us spreads everywhere the fragrance of the knowledge of him. For we are to God the aroma of Christ among those who are being saved and those who are perishing. To the one, we are the smell of death; to the other, the fragrance of life. And who is equal to such a task? (2 Corinthians 2:14-16)"

Furthermore, freshness comes by staying whole with God. Wholeness comes by your life becoming a garden of God's grace. Natural gardens decay, but a seasoned spiritual life bears much fruit. Keep out the weeds of the world and the seeds of sin. Then you are positioned to finish well with a fresh and fruitful faith. Middle and old age is not for complaining, but for proclaiming the goodness of God.

Joseph stayed fresh and patient. As a result, the fruit of his life flourished the older he became (Genesis 49:22). Aged believers possess ripe experiences and a track record of God's trustworthiness. So stay fresh in your faith. Keep your garden of grace growing. Stay watered with the Word.

The effects of staying fresh are compounding. Overtime the outward man decays, but the inner man grows strong. The Bible says, "Therefore we do not lose heart. Though outwardly we are wasting away, yet inwardly we are being renewed day by day. For our light and momentary troubles are achieving for us an eternal glory that far outweighs them all (2 Corinthians 4:16-17)." God's work of grace keeps you fresh. He preserves believers to the end. Though declining, you are climbing higher and higher with Christ.

Therefore, stay fresh by submitting to your Savior. Stay fresh by feeding your soul fresh bread from the Bible. Stay fresh by investing in those who have yet to taste the grace of God. Stay fresh by trying new things and being around new believers. Stay fresh as a student of God and people. Fresh faith flourishes in fruit bearing. Freshness keeps you young at heart and keen in mind. Stay fresh and aging becomes your ally!

REFLECTIONS

_____

_____

_____

_____

_____

_____

TENACIOUS TRUTH

Your statutes stand firm, holiness adorns your house for endless days, O Lord.
Psalm 93:5

The statutes of God stand firm, forever. No secular storm can blow His truth from its moorings. No tempest of deceptive lies can un-tether truth from Almighty God. As the rocks remain unmoved from the tumult of the raging seas, so does God's truth resist the shifting current of culture's opinions. Our faith is not founded on a fable, but on the foundation of God's character. What He says can be trusted and acted upon, because He is 100% trustworthy. The obedient centurion (Matthew 8:13) experienced this.

When Jesus spoke, he believed and his servant was immediately healed. Indeed, healing comes as you heed the words of Jesus. Do not hesitate to embrace the words of God and prolong your pain. Believe what He says, and do what He says. His truth is your thermostat for living. Make God your gage for behavior. His truth is eternal and dependable.

Furthermore, thank God for the outcomes of His truth. His truth sets you free (John 8:32). His truth protects you (Psalm 40:11). His truth guides you (Psalm 25:5). His truth allows you to persevere (Proverbs 12:19). His truth creates value (Proverbs 16:13). His truth facilitates our worship (John 4:24). His truth is to be obeyed (Galatians 5:7). His truth is to be loved (I Thessalonians 2:10). His truth leads to thanksgiving (I Timothy 4:3).

His truth brings joy (3 John 1:4). You can be extremely grateful to God for the fruit of His truth. Do not take truth for granted, but remain grateful instead. Stay a student of truth. This sends a signal of what you value and appreciate. The truth of God is a tremendous asset. Thank God for His truth. Praise the Lord for His precepts. His statutes stand firm.

Lastly, allow the truth of Almighty God to transform your mind and heart. Be transformed by the renewing of your mind (Romans 12:2). Keep your mind tidy with truth. Otherwise, your mind becomes cluttered and confused with messy thinking. Invite Christ's truth to clean up the home of your heart. Then your heart will be furnished with the fixtures of His truth. Holiness will adorn your character and life. Right thinking and pure living is the goal of understanding and applying knowledge and truth.

Your pride is meant to deflate and your humility inflate, under the influence of God's truth. Allow tenacious truth to take hold of your soul. His truth is an antidote to sin's deception. His truth never exits, even if ignored. You can return to truth, because it never left. Tenacious truth is your true north. Bend towards truth. Embrace truth. Believe truth. Obey truth. Be transformed by truth. It is your faith's firm foundation!

REFLECTIONS

_____

_____

_____

_____

_____

_____

78

CHRIST'S CONSOLATION

When anxiety was great within me, your consolation brought joy to my soul.
Psalm 94:19

Anxiety can overwhelm us. It can feel overwhelming like an imposing mountain too high to climb, or it can be smothering like being trapped under the sea. An anxious heart is impossible to handle alone. It will continue to eat away at your peace and security until you are totally consumed by fear and failure. Anxiety kills relationships, because there is nothing left to give. Your emotional capacity is sucked dry with worry.

People tend to avoid the anxious, because they feel preyed upon. Perpetual anxiety becomes relational dead weight. No one is immune to anxiety, as the wise and the wealthy Solomon stated, "An anxious heart weighs a man down, but a kind word cheers him up" (Proverbs 12:25).

Sometimes anxiety attacks you from the rear of a relationship. You believe things are going just fine right before it blows up in your face. You feel rejected and totally out of control. This is your time to refrain from attacking back and retreat with Christ. Replace anxiety and anger with trust and patience. Patience follows love. You are patient with the things you love. Love is patient (I Corinthians 13:4).

Allow the Lord to love on you, so you can love on others. Christ is your counselor. He replaces your hurt with forgiveness. He transforms your sorrow with hope. He leads you out of rejection into His sanctuary of rest. Let your heart go there. The counsel of Christ brings joy to your soul.

The joy of Jesus is your jumping off point in prayer. The comfort of Christ generates joy. Your extreme anxiety is God's opportunity. Your comfort flows out of your communion with Christ. Have a little talk with Jesus. Tell Him all about your problems. Bye and bye, you will say goodbye to anxious thinking and replace it with joyful trust. You become giddy with God when you know He is in control. Have faith in His attributes of mercy and power.

Indeed, Christ consoles you, so you can console others. You are a pass through for God's grace. Do not strive anxiously. Instead, go to God for grace and dispense it liberally. You will be glad you did, and so will those around you who anxiously wait. An ounce of grace is weightier than a ton of anxiety. Do not be anxious about anything (Philippians 4:12). Leave it with the Lord, and receive the joy of the Lord. He is your soul's strength!

REFLECTIONS

_____

_____

_____

_____

_____

_____

79

HEART ISSUES

Today if you hear his voice, do not harden your hearts as you did in Meribah,
as you did that day at Massah in the desert..."
Psalm 95:7b-8

A hardened heart cannot hear. It chooses not to listen. It is obstinately and constantly ignorant to the ways of God. Its mind is made up to meander down the path of pride. A hardened heart wanders the wrong way (Hebrews 3:10). Furthermore, it is hurtful. It inflicts pain on itself and others. A hardened heart fossilizes faith.

It builds up layers of hurt that encrust into stubbornness over time. It is trapped in a web of mistrust and misdeeds. Humans harden hearts, but only heaven can soften them. It is the tender touch of Jesus that moistens a man's heart. His love lubricates. He infuses humility.

Indeed, the cure for a hardened heart is humility. A humble heart moves from a stubborn soul to a sensitive spirit. It grows from immaturity to maturity. It migrates from going its own way to following God's way. Humility hoses hardness with healing. Humility softens hardness. Humility is liquid love. It moistens the dry clay of a crusty heart. It softens under the caring and caressing hands of Christ.

He is the potter and you are the clay. Clay humbly submits to its creator (Isaiah 29:16). Humility keeps you moldable and useable. Otherwise, pride cracks under pressure. It becomes brittle and loses its boldness. However, humility positions you to become the artwork of Almighty God. You become beautiful to behold.

Therefore, humble yourself under the mighty hand of God (I Peter 5:6). Do it today in preparation for tomorrow. Pride procrastinates. Humility activates. Your humility will ratchet up exponentially your capacity and ability for listening. Then you can listen large. Listen to the Lord's voracious voice of wisdom. Listen to your caring spouse's voice of concern. Listen to your mentor's mature voice of warnings and reminders. Listen quietly to your humbled heart. Listen below its hardened superficial surface, and listen to its softened sensitive side.

Christ is calling you back. He is the shepherd of your sheep-like soul. Moreover, do not give up on the hard-hearted. Continue to pursue them with persistent prayer, care and accountability. Be bold, but loving. Be courageous, but caring. Above all else, give them over to God. He is whom they ultimately answer. Hardened hearts need heaven's healing. A humble heart hears the Lord, loud and clear!

REFLECTIONS

_____

_____

_____

_____

_____

_____

80

HIS HOLINESS

Worship the Lord in the splendor of his holiness;
tremble before him, all the earth.
Psalm 96:9

Holiness is the glorious combination of God's attributes. It sums up His comprehensive character. No wonder it is overwhelming. God's holiness is a beautiful sight to behold. It is splendor in the sight of his saints. Holiness is attractive. Indeed, it is in our worship that we appreciate the Almighty for who He is. He is our awesome God. He is high and lifted up. Like Isaiah we are overwhelmed by the grandeur of His greatness and glory.

"I saw the Lord seated on a throne, high and exalted, and the train of his robe filled the temple" (Isaiah 6:1). Kings die and are deposed, but our King reigns forever. His eternal throne towers above the temporary monarchs of men. His holiness is regal, yet raw in reality.

As we perceive the enormity of His holiness, we pray and worship in profound awe of the Almighty. If earthly kings engage our respect and honor, how much more should the King of Kings? John felt this on the isle of Patmos. The Bible describes the surreal effect of heaven's holiness on a mere human being, "When I saw him, I fell at his feet as though dead. Then he placed his right hand on me and said: "Do not be afraid. I am the First and the Last. I am the Living One; I was dead, and behold I am alive for ever and ever! And I hold the keys of death and Hades" (Revelation 1:17-18).

God's holiness adjusts our posture. It alters our lives. Therefore, ascribe to Almighty God the glory due His name. Speak the Lord's name with holy reverence and fear. Do not speak of God glibly. Allow His holiness to make you attractive with character beautiful to behold.

It is in the presence of Holy God that you are convicted of unholy attitudes, actions and conversations. Therefore, let the language from His pure lips lead you to love with your words. Look into the compelling eyes of His concern, and allow Him to create a countenance of compassion on your face. Grab hold of His eager hands to help, and have them hold you accountable to serve others with your gifts and generosity. His holiness is a mega motivator for your holiness. He says to be holy as He is holy (I Peter 1:15-16).

Without the grace of God we are ugly to behold. We are deformed and undone. However, the Holy Spirit surprises you with beauty. He executes an extreme makeover of your soul and spirit. Your life is made lovely under the transforming power of Holy God. His holiness is your asset of attractiveness. Behold His beauty and become beautiful. Worship the Lord in the splendor of His holiness!

REFLECTIONS

_____

_____

_____

_____

_____

_____

81

BE GLAD

The Lord reigns, let the earth be glad; let the distant shores rejoice.
Psalm 97:1

You can be glad, because the Lord reigns. He reigns over the righteous and the unrighteous. God governs the universe. Christ is in control. Jesus said, "All authority in heaven and on earth has been given to me" (Matthew 28:18). Therefore, He is who every man or woman must submit to in obedient faith. Our God reigns. These are comforting words to those of us who follow Christ.

Only those who reject or forget Jesus recoil from His reign. They live in a sad state. Indeed, there is great joy and comfort knowing Christ is on His throne. The reign of earthly rulers can be ruinous and unrighteous, but the reign of God gives life and righteousness. Be glad that God governs by grace and with power.

Your life may seem little right now. You feel faithless, overwhelmed, and beaten down by a barrage of disbelief, problems and misconceptions. Lies linger too long and do not tell you the truth. They are confusing. Sadness is seeping into your soul. You may feel taken advantage of, or misunderstood. Your life seems to be swirling out of control. Your faith may be fractured under the unfair weight of the world. Don't despair.

There is good news. Your Heavenly Father has not been deposed by the devil. Satan cannot usurp the authority of Almighty God. The kingdoms of this world are full of injustice, crimes and punishment. However, the Kingdom of God is just, freeing and rewarding. Bow in belief to King Jesus. He will dispense hope and joy to your hurting heart. God gives gladness.

Jesus prayed, "Your kingdom come, your will be done on earth as it is in heaven..." (Matthew 6:10). God's will is for Him to reign in His saints and through His saints. His followers are to engage as Kingdom citizens. He spoke through the prophet Daniel, "Then the sovereignty, power and greatness of the kingdoms under the whole heaven will be handed over to the saints, the people of the Most High. His kingdom will be an everlasting kingdom, and all rulers will worship and obey him" (Daniel 7:27).

Be glad, for there is coming the day when His people will reign exclusively over His kingdom. Be glad, you are not of this world, though you are in the world as His representative. Be glad, you are God's. Be glad, He reigns over life and death. Be glad... He is your King!

REFLECTIONS

_____

_____

_____

_____

_____

_____

82

BE JOYFUL

Let the rivers clap their hands, let the mountains sing together for joy;
let them sing before the Lord, for he comes to judge the earth. He will judge
the world in righteousness and the peoples with equity.
Psalm 98:8-9

Is judgment escorted by joy? Yes, for the Lord's earth and for Jesus' followers they walk hand in hand. Almighty God's judgment is accompanied by the joy of His handiwork. Therefore, celebrate Christ's coming. Celebrate His first coming for He has done marvelous things. His life was matchless in the application of pure virtue. His death was sacrificially in providing salvation for all who believe. His resurrection was electric in releasing eternal energy for all who are filled by His Holy Spirit.

There is an overflowing fountain of joy from His first coming. Furthermore, celebrate His second coming. He will judge everyone righteously and with equity. The judgment of Jesus is joyful, because it makes right. You can rejoice because of the righteous judgment of God. Joyful surrender means you are ready for Christ's coming. Indeed, Jesus' mother, Mary, embraced this reality.

Mary understood joy at the first coming of Jesus. After the angel's words sunk in that she was to become a mom, the mother of God, she exclaimed, "My soul glorifies the Lord, and my soul rejoices in God my Savior" (Luke 1:46-47). Becoming a mother gyrated her soul with joy. Baby Jesus was her joy. She could not keep quiet for the coming of her Lord and her child was at hand. Joy resonated in the heavens, and resounded throughout all the earth. It was Christ's coming out party.

Joy was the outcome of His incoming. Mary was surprised by joy. Indeed, motherhood brings joy. Great pain is followed by an even greater joy (John 16:21). Children, teens and adult children still cause pain, but don't let them steal your joy. Make sure your security and significance is in Christ and not in your son or daughter. Your identity is in Christ. Your Savior defines your success. Make sure you go to Christ for a cup of joy. Drink often. The Lord's joy is limitless.

Above all else, live your life in triumphant victory, not in dismal defeat. You are more than conquerors through Christ, through Him that loves you (Romans 8:37). The Lord's great love is your life preserver. The joy of the Lord is your strength (Nehemiah 8:10). You serve a risen Savior who is in the world today. By God's grace your business or ministry will make payroll. Be patient and persevere in prayer for your prodigal child or friend. They may one day grow sick of sin.

Do not allow mistreatment or inequities to rob your joy. God will one day judge with equity. His days seem longer than ours, so be patient. Turn off the depressing songs of Satan. He is a joy killer. Reject His joyless tunes. Instead, tune in to your trustworthy Savior Jesus. Sing at the top of your lungs to the Lord. Sing the new song Christ has composed. His Holy Spirit harmonizes your life with joy and peace. So sing. Sing for you are joyful for what He has done. Sing for you are joyful for what He is doing. Sing for you are joyful for what He will do. The coming judgment of Jesus brings joy to Jesus' followers. Radically rejoice. Be joyful in Jesus!

REFLECTIONS

_____

_____

_____

_____

_____

_____

83

PRAYING LEADERS

Moses and Aaron were among his priests, Samuel was among those
who called on his name; they called on the Lord and he answered them.
Psalm 99:6

Why do leaders need to pray? Leaders need to pray, because they can substitute their successes for supplication to their Savior. Also, they are most susceptible to taking matters into their own hands and forgetting heaven. Moreover, they can drive so hard that they hinder the work of the Holy Spirit. Leaders are also great candidates for prayer, because they are out front and exposed to the enemy.

They need prayer's protection. In distress the devil tempts them. In success, pride seduces them. Leaders need to look to the Lord for He is their all-knowing leader. Paul, on the road to Damascus, was arrested by Almighty God's grace. Blinded by the light of God's leadership, he followed not totally sure of the reason or the results (Acts 22:9-11). Leaders need prayer because God's plan is much bigger than their brain alone can comprehend.

Furthermore, praying leaders have a profound impact on those around them. They rub off on others the residue of prayer: faith, hope, love, grace, forgiveness, purity and courage. It is on bended knee you gain the wisdom, confidence and creditability to then stand and lead. Learning to lead comes out of the discipline of prayer. Prayer protects you from running too far, too fast. Prayer restrains you from racing ahead of the Lord. In the upper room, after the life transforming resurrection and ascension of Christ, the disciples prayed over a leadership need (Acts 1:14).

The Lord led them into a wise decision and filled them with the Holy Spirit to serve. Indeed, prayer reins you in to get ready, or it releases you to accomplish radical results for His glory. Leaders petition the Lord for large things. They pray for entire nations to fall to their knees in acknowledgement of Almighty God.

Lastly, praying leaders pronounce their utter dependence on God. You pray like you breathe, often and unconsciously. However, when the heart rate of your soul accelerates, your prayers become more obvious and public. Therefore, invest the time to pray with and for your team. Prayer breathes life. It is your first offensive tactic, not your last resort. Prayer is not your plan B. Prayer is always plan A. Gather together often your family to pray for the sick, the lost and those leaders in authority (I Timothy 2:1-3).

Pray when you feel led. Pray when you don't feel led. The effect of your prayers is not based on your feelings, but on faith. Indeed, the level and intensity of your followers' prayers, rarely exceeds the prayers of you the leader. So, pray believing your prayers will lead others to pray. Your prayers do elevate everyone else's prayers. Above all else, praying leaders see God act!

REFLECTIONS

_____

_____

_____

_____

_____

_____

84

ENDURING LOVE

For the Lord is good and his love endures forever;
his faithfulness continues through all generations.
Psalm 100:5

The love of God never ceases. Christ's love is continual because it flows from the inexhaustible reservoir of God's goodness. Man's lakes can languish for lack of rain, but not the love of the Lord. There is no drought of love in the divine scheme of things. It rains down from heaven in massive sheets of mercy and faithfulness. It pelts our pride and melts our heart. The love of God endures. Your Heavenly Father's love is not fickle. It is faithful and true.

Your earthly father's love may be conditional and undependable. It may be hard for him to love, because he has not been loved. But. you have the opportunity and privilege of moving beyond the drought of your dad's love, and bowing beneath the bowels of Christ's compassion. Christ's covenant of love with His children never alters. You can trust God's unfailing love for forever and forever (Psalm 52:8).

Therefore, because of God's enduring love, you have reason to rejoice. His love is your excuse to exercise enormous and ongoing praise and thanksgiving. Do not remain defeated by dire circumstances and negative thinking. God loves you. He has saved your soul. God loves you. He has made you whole. God loves you. He provides you work. God loves you. He has given you life. God loves you.

Indeed, it is important that you have full understanding of every good thing God has given you (Philemon 1:6). When this occurs you cannot help but exclaim His goodness and mercy. Your shouts of joy drown out the murmurings meandering in your mind. You are His. 'Owned by God' is your trademark of trust. Let gratitude govern your thinking, because God's love endures forever.

Because His love is everlasting, you have Christ's capacity to continually love through you. You can love sinners and saints alike. Jesus did (Luke 5:30). He spent time with people unlike Himself. This is the posture of love. During this

Christmas season make sure you reach out and love on the unlovable. Be patient, kind and forgiving toward family members who don't have a clue of what Christ has done for them. Love them, even when they are hard to understand. Love them in spite of their unfair criticism and surly sarcasm.

Release God's love to shine through your soul. Be a leader of love. You know better. Your love will make a lasting impression on your parents and on your children. It is Christ's love, manifested through you, that the Lord uses to lead others to Himself. Be a love leader who endures. Love during the good times and especially the hard times. Love endures!

REFLECTIONS

_____

_____

_____

_____

_____

_____

85

EYE PROTECTION

I walk in my house with blameless heart. I will set my eyes before no vile thing.
The deeds of faithless men I hate; they will not cling to me.
Psalm 101:2b-3

Spiritual eyesight is a gift from God. It is beautiful to behold. His Spirit allows us to see and understand spiritual truths (I Corinthians 2:12-14). This is why we want our walk with Christ to be blameless. A blameless life is able to behold Almighty God and His attributes. A blameless life keeps your eyesight from becoming blurred to your Savior. It sees the goodness of God above the wickedness of the world.

Moreover, the object of its faith focus begins at home. Your home is where your heart is revealed. It is here that you need your Heavenly Father the most. Watch well. Where your eyes give permission the heart gives admission. Eve and Adam were first fixated by the appeal of the fruit on their eyes (Genesis 3:6-7). Their eyes were opened by sin to sin. Once its allure entered their eyes. it arrested their mind and hand. They ignored protecting their eyes. Eye protection is essential to enter into a close walk with Christ. It honors Him. It helps your home.

Furthermore, hatred of sin is an effective sentinel for the door of virtue. Do not flirt with sin; instead view it with scorn and abhorrence. Christ died for our sins (I Corinthians 15:3). The least we can do is die to sin. Paul was a good example of this. By faith, he died daily (I Corinthians 15:31 KJV). Abundant life (John 10:10 KJV) is preceded by redundant death. The sirens of sin will seduce you more often than not. Avoid what you see coming. Stay away from online sites that are suggestive.

Install software that monitors your activity. Ask trusted friends to review the report of your web activity. This is wisdom. Moreover, use television as a tool for good and not evil. Set a goal to spend more time reading instructional and inspirational books, than watching TV. Shun evil. Entertain and embrace eternal matters, over evil delights. Wicked sight causes you to wander from your Savior. However, eye protection is an invitation to walk with Christ.

Therefore, only fascinate your eyes with what is acceptable to your Heavenly Father. He is serious about how you steward your eyesight (Matthew 5:29). Your eyes are a paintbrush to the canvas of your soul. Use both of them to create works of art, pleasing to the Almighty. This inner artwork is attractive to those who matter to you the most. Nonetheless, be wise where you look. Look on God's creation with awe and admiration.

Look on the poor with generosity and care. Look on the lost with compassion and prayer. Look on your family with patience, love and forgiveness. Look on the church for worship, service and teaching. Where you look is where you go. Where you look is what you become. So, be selective and protective with your eyes. Your eyes are the entrance of all things, good or bad. Focus on the good. Have an eye for the eternal. Above all else, look to the Lord first and foremost!

REFLECTIONS

86

CRY FOR HELP

Hear my prayer, O Lord; let my cry for help come to you.
Psalm 102:1

Sometimes you feel desperate. Your needs get the best of you and they overwhelm you. Your sorrow has intensified your prayers into crying. But, this is the design of distress. It is meant to drive you to God. You cry out to Christ, because He cares. Seek heaven for help. It is here that you have the radical resources for right living.

It is here your troubled soul can be soothed. Trouble finds trust and peace in Christ (John 14:1-6). You find security with your Savior. A cry for help is humbling, but it is not meant to be humiliating. It is those who refuse help who look foolish. Wisdom cries out to God. It acknowledges the Almighty. Therefore, seek often the kind face of your Heavenly Father.

Indeed, do not allow your private woes, your personal enemies, or your physical aliments to drive a wedge between you and God. Pause in your painful lamentation and earnestly seek the Lord. Your complaint to Christ will not be held against you. It is here you release your anger and receive God's grace. The person with whom you have conflict may never change, but you can.

Receive God's love, so you can love. Receive God's forgiveness, so you can forgive. Receive Christ's courage, so you can be courageous. Receive the joy of Jesus, so you can be joyful. Receive heaven's hope, so you can be hopeful. There is weeping in the night, but joy comes in the morning (Psalm 30:5).

Lastly, sincere supplication to your Savior is your aggressive ally. Use it for yourself and others. Furthermore, do not be shy about acquainting others with your grief. Do not struggle through life bearing your burdens alone (Galatians 6:2). It becomes a blessing for some to be your burden bearer. Christians are meant to live in community, and not in the silent cries of isolation.

Indeed, your transparent confession aligns your heart with other hurting hearts. Your current cries are building your relational resume for future ministry. By God's grace you will one day soon be able to walk with someone else through a similar circumstance. Grief does not get the last word, God does. His Word heals you (Psalm 107:20), so you can be a conduit for others who cry out to Christ. Listen pensively to the pain in others. Cradle their cries in your prayers and lift them to heaven. The Lord listens to your cries. He cares. He loves. He woos you to wipe away your tears!

REFLECTIONS

87

BENEFITS PACKAGE

Praise the Lord, O my soul, and forget not all his benefits—
Psalm 103:2

God's benefits package is exceedingly generous. It is not limited to human resources, but is supported by heaven resources. God is your HR (heaven resources) Director. He forgives your sins and gives you eternal life insurance. His sick leave includes healing from disease. He rescues you from the pit of purposeless living and places you into a caring community with convictions. He crowns you with love and compassion. He satisfies your longings with good things.

He renews your energy, so you can engage life with tenacious abandonment. God's benefits to believers' way exceed what you deserve. This is music to the ears of your soul. It causes you to burst forth in praise, 'Bless the Lord, O my soul.' This contains more gratitude to God than your tongue alone can tell. You may be like Moses; you are so inundated by His benefits you have to request relief from His blessings (Exodus 36:5-6). His bountiful benefits can overwhelm you.

Therefore, pray for wisdom on how to manage God's blessings. Make it mandatory to remember all of His benefits. If not, your memory can become treacherous about the best things. Do not lock away in solitude your answered prayers by the Almighty. Remember the spouse you prayed for and how God gave you much more than you deserved. You are the benefactor for life of a companion who cares for you like Christ. Moreover, how beneficial is the job He has given you? It is not perfect, but it is perfect for you. Your role at work is a platform for Kingdom influence. Steward it well. Serve unselfishly. Indeed, His benefits are a treasure entrusted to you. Use His benefits for the benefit of others. This was Joseph's posture when his family was in need. He invited them to benefit from his position of influence and success. He provided for them abundantly (Genesis 42).

Lastly, bless Him who blesses you. Otherwise benefits taken for granted lose their luster. Dissatisfied entitlement replaces gratitude. Furthermore, maintain a prayerful perspective. See your circumstances as beneficial to you becoming better. Take on the attributes of Almighty God. You are meant to become like His benefits of holiness, love, forgiveness, mercy, compassion, and grace. His benefits make you better. Yes, they are to be enjoyed, but they are also to be engrafted into your being.

Paul out of personal experience writes, "And we rejoice in the hope of the glory of God. Not only so, but we also rejoice in our sufferings, because we know that suffering produces perseverance; perseverance, character; and character, hope. And hope does not disappoint us, because God has poured out his love into our hearts by the Holy Spirit, whom he has given us" (Romans 5:2b-5). His benefits are bold and life changing. His benefits package is robust and real. It eagerly and excessively exceeds the world's standards. Therefore, from the depths of your soul, bless the Lord and forget not all His benefits!

REFLECTIONS

_____

_____

_____

_____

_____

_____

88

GLADDEN THE HEART

He makes grass grow for the cattle, and plants for man to cultivate—
bringing forth food from the earth: wine that gladdens the heart of man,
oil to make his face shine, and bread that sustains the heart.
Psalm 104:14-15

Wine is meant by God to gladden the heart. It originates from the fruit of His creation. Jesus made wine at the wedding of a friend (John 2:3-11). This was the first of His miracles. It caused His disciples to place their faith in Him. Indeed, wine is for times of celebration and merriment. It is to be used responsibly. Discipline and self-control are assigned as its escorts. Therefore, be wise about wine.

Do not partake if it will cause a brother to stumble (Romans 14:21). Responsibility and maturity do not tempt others. It also abstains in deference to those who abstain. Wine's design is to make the heart merry, but not to inebriate the mind. It is enjoyed in moderation and not in drunkenness (Ephesians 5:18). Instead, allow Christ to control your life through the filling of His Spirit.

Furthermore, leaders are to lead an exemplary life of non-excessive wine drinking. Paul described this standard to Timothy for church leaders. "Deacons, likewise, are to be men worthy of respect, sincere, not indulging in much wine, and not pursuing dishonest gain" (I Timothy 3:8). Even effective leaders like Noah were embarrassed by drink. He became drunk on wine (Genesis 9:21). His lapse in judgment lost him respect.

Indeed, alcohol causes you to lose your inhibitions that can lead to unsavory behavior. This is why wisdom enjoys wine with accountability. Don't drink if it can lead you into temptation. The wise use of wine is limited, or none at all. Avoid its blessing becoming a curse. If you are a leader, be extremely cautious. One bad night could stain a lifetime of respect.

Lastly, use your freedom to drink, or not to drink with humility and sensitivity. In either case it doesn't make you any more spiritual. Pride from not drinking wine is as ugly as drunkenness from drinking wine. Do not lord your freedom in either direction, over those who believe differently. God's good creation is not to be polluted by either. Your' preferences are not to be treated like convictions.

Preferences vary from person to person. Convictions are constant and consistent in Christ followers. Moreover, Paul told Timothy to take a little wine for his illness (I Timothy 5:23). A medicinal purpose is another option to use wine wisely. So, as the Lord leads enjoy the fruit of the vine. Allow God to gladden your heart through the wise use of wine. Be discreet. Be accountable. Be glad!

REFLECTIONS

_____

_____

_____

_____

_____

_____

89

POSITION OF INFLUENCE

He made him [Joseph] master of his household, ruler over all he possessed,
to instruct his princes as he pleased and teach his elders wisdom.
Psalm 105:21-22

You are in a position of influence for a purpose. A significant part of your purpose is to influence influencers. Like Joseph, God may have positioned you in a place you could not have scripted alone. He has taken your troubled circumstances and turned them into an opportunity for good. Because you were faithful during the stressful times, He has opened a door of robust responsibility. Don't shrink back from this new role.

Instead, remember where you once were: In need of an advocate and mentor. Pray for those around you, with whom you can invest your wisdom and time. Leaders need godly counselors they can trust (Proverbs 15:22). Wisdom is their ally that leads them into success. Furthermore, your character is your greatest credentials. It leads others to listen.

Therefore, stay humble and teachable. Engage in the engrafting of God's word into your heart and mind. If you are not growing your soul shrivels and eventually atrophies. You earn the right to be respected and followed, as you submit to Almighty God and the authorities in your life. Joseph was falsely accused and mistreated, but he kept the high road of submission to the process, until the truth prevailed. He trusted God for equity and justice. It was his resourceful response to injustice that won him the respect of his peers and those in control.

In the same way you have the opportunity to whine, or win over the hearts of others with your trusting heart. Use your position of influence to first and foremost point people to Christ. Start with the small circle of those who know you best and then watch the Lord leverage your influence into a grandeur scale for His glory. Authorities invite influence from those with whom they trust. Stay trustworthy in the small things and the larger ones will take care of themselves (Matthew 25:21).

Lastly, see your influence as a stewardship and steward it well. Don't take it lightly. It marks them for life when you regularly tell your child, "I am so proud of you. God is using you." Or, when you remark to your spouse, "I love you. Thank you for who you are and all you do for our family. You mean the world to me." Perhaps it is a hand written note to a friend that expresses your admiration for their example and/or gratitude for their generosity. Influencers speak lovingly and truthful about others. They influence and earn the right for more influence when they influence well.

Above all else, be influenced by God through embedding His Word into your heart (Psalm 119:10-11). Make prayer a priority to listen to the Lord and do what He says. The most effective influencers are those who are influenced by the Almighty, and by those who fear Him. Be an example of integrity and your influence will never lack the Lord's blessing. Influence is purposeful!

REFLECTIONS

_____

_____

_____

_____

_____

_____

90

CONSISTENT BEHAVIOR

Blessed are they who maintain justice, who constantly do what is right."
Psalm 106:3

Consistent behavior brings out the blessing of God and incurs the favor of man. Right living sounds an "amen" from your Savior. Yes, there will be those who snarl at your good works, but this is to be expected. Not everyone is interested in integrity, but most people do respect what is right. Proud men punished Daniel, because he did what was right with his persistent prayers (Daniel 6:10-12).

Indeed, it is better to constantly pray to Christ and receive clarity, than to stay confused with inconsistent intercession. Constant prayer keeps you aware of the Almighty's agenda, for it is your 'check and balance' to good behavior. Be constantly in the presence of Christ and you can conform to the truth that you are wholly His. The Lord's ownership requires holiness, embrace this principle and it will bring happiness to your humble heart. Christ blesses your regular right living.

Secondly, constantly do right and you will grow the equity of your integrity. Consistent character gives you the 'card' of creditability, respect and influence. For instance, follow through with your word, especially when circumstances change. If you quoted someone a sell price, or made a generous promise to a friend, follow through even though the facts may have shifted out of your favor. Relationships are more important than a few dollars, or even when you deserve better. Your consistent behavior may be what wins them over to Christ.

It is costly to constantly do what is right, but it can bankrupt your robust reputation if you submit to inconsistency. Your children need your behavior to be consistent, so they can feel secure. Your team expects consistency, so they are not derailed or discouraged by your ever-changing character. Integrity is not inconsistent, but double mindedness is a deterrent of the devil. James explains it well, "For let not that man expect that he will receive anything from the Lord, being a double-minded man, unstable in all his ways" (James 1:7-8, NASB). Single-mindedness brings stability.

Lastly, define and do right as outlined by Almighty God. Christ's concordance of right is laid out in Holy Writ. "It is written" (Matthew 4:4) was a constant phrase that seasoned the lips of Jesus. He quoted Scripture in teaching and conversations, because it was His baseline for belief and behavior. Therefore, appeal to your detractors by humbly deferring to the Bible as the motive behind your consistent behavior. Adhere to the Almighty's words and you will effectively do His work.

Beware of not treating the Lord's principles like a cafeteria buffet, by only selecting what 'fits your fancy'. Conform to Christ's character and not to the world's wishy-washy way of living. Constantly doing right is not always fun, but it is freeing when you look into the face of Jesus with no regrets. Do justly at all times, and you will see Jesus smile. By God's grace, constantly do what is right and people will see Jesus in you. Your consistent behavior brings about blessing!

REFLECTIONS

_____

_____

_____

_____

_____

_____

How To Become a Disciple of Jesus Christ

"Then Jesus came to them and said,
"All authority in heaven and on earth has been given to me.
Therefore go and make disciples of all nations, baptizing them
in the name of the Father and of the Son and of the Holy Spirit,
and teaching them to obey everything I have commanded you.
And surely I am with you always, to the very end of the age"
(Matthew 28:18-20).

*Holy Scripture gives us principles related to becoming
a disciple and to making disciples:*

1. BELIEVE

"That if you confess with your mouth, "Jesus is Lord," and believe in your heart
that God raised him from the dead, you will be saved" (Romans 10:9).

Belief in Jesus Christ as your Savior and Lord gives you eternal life in heaven.

2. REPENT AND BE BAPTIZED

"Peter replied, "Repent and be baptized, every one of you, in the name of Jesus
Christ for the forgiveness of your sins. And you will receive the gift of the Holy Spirit"
(Acts 2:38).

*Repentance means you turn from you sin and
then publicly confess Christ in baptism.*

3. OBEY

"Jesus replied, "If anyone loves me, he will obey my teaching. My Father will love him,
and we will come to him and make our home with him" (John 14:23).

Obedience is an indicator of our love for the Lord Jesus and His presence in our life.

4. WORSHIP, PRAYER, COMMUNITY, EVANGELISM AND STUDY

"Every day they continued to meet together in the temple courts.
They broke bread in their homes and ate together with glad and sincere hearts,
praising God and enjoying the favor of all the people. And the Lord added
to their number daily those who were being saved" (Acts 2:46-47).

*Worship and prayer is our expression of gratitude and honor to God and
our dependence on His grace. Community and evangelism is accountability
to Christians and compassion for non-Christians. Study to apply the knowledge,
understanding and wisdom of God.*

5. LOVE GOD

"Jesus replied: " 'Love the Lord your God with all your heart and with all your
soul and with all your mind.' This is the first and greatest commandment"
(Matthew 22:37-38).

*Intimacy with Almighty God is a growing and loving relationship. We are loved
by Him, so we can love others and be empowered by the Holy Spirit to obey
His commands.*

6. LOVE PEOPLE

"And the second is like it: 'Love your neighbor as yourself"
(Matthew 22:39).

*Loving people is an outflow of the love for our Heavenly Father.
We are able to love because He first loved us.*

7. MAKE DISCIPLES

"And the things you have heard me say in the presence of many witnesses
entrust to reliable men who will also be qualified to teach others"
(2 Timothy 2:2).

*The reason we disciple others is because we are extremely grateful to God
and to those who disciple us, and we want to obey Christ's last instructions
before going to heaven.*

About The Author

Boyd Bailey enjoys the role of Chief Encouragement Officer at Ministry Ventures, a company he co-founded in 1999. His passion is to encourage and equip leaders engaged in Kingdom focused enterprises. Since 2004 he has also served as President and founder of Wisdom Hunters, a ministry that seeks to connect people to Christ through devotional writing—with over 60,000 daily email readers.

Ministry Ventures has trained approximately 1,000 faith-based non-profits and coached for certification over 100 ministries in the best practices of prayer, board development, ministry model, administration and fundraising. By God's grace over $30 million has been raised through the ministries served and thousands of people led into a growing relationship with Jesus Christ.

Prior to Ministry Ventures, Boyd was the National Director for Crown Financial Ministries. He was instrumental in the expansion of Crown into 30 major markets across the U.S. He was a key facilitator in the $25 million merger between Christian Financial Concepts and Crown Ministries.

Before his work with Crown, Boyd and Andy Stanley started First Baptist Atlanta's north campus, and, as an elder, Boyd assisted Andy in the start of North Point Community Church. In college he bought a service company with five employees. This business endeavor financed his education and the equity from its sale was the economic launching pad for his graduate school experience.

Boyd Lee Bailey was born in 1960, in Huntsville, Alabama and received his bachelor of arts from Jacksonville State University and his Masters of Divinity from Southwestern Seminary in Ft. Worth, Texas. Boyd and his wife Rita live in Roswell, Georgia. They have been married 32 years and are blessed with four daughters and three sons-in-law who love Jesus. He and Rita are most excited about new grandchildren Lillian (2 years) and Hudson (7 months)!

Boyd serves on the boards of Ministry Ventures, Wisdom Hunters and Blue Print for Life. He and his wife Rita join three other couples every two weeks for accountability and fellowship around their marriages. Boyd enjoys reading the classics, business trends, theology, and electronic news, books and magazines.

He and Rita like to hike, travel, sit by the fire in the mountains, enjoy a cup of coffee at home and walk on the beach. Missions, travel and college football are passions as well. What's most enjoyable is to get quiet before the Lord in prayer.